THE
EVERYDAY
GUIDE TO...
THE GOSPELS

DEDICATION

For my sister and brother in Christ
Dorothy and Chuck Booher

". . .that God may be All in all."
1 CORINTHIANS 15:28

THE EVERYDAY GUIDE TO...
THE GOSPELS

DANIEL PARTNER

HUMBLECREEK
INSPIRATION FOR LIFE

Published by Humble Creek, P.O. Box 719, Uhrichsville, Ohio 44683

Printed in the United States of America.
5 4 3 2 1

Contents

Preface 7
Introduction to the Gospel of Matthew 9
Study of Matthew 10
Answer Key to Questions in Matthew 77
Introduction to the Gospel of Mark 81
Study of Mark 82
Answer Key to Questions in Mark 113
Introduction to the Gospel of Luke 115
Study of Luke 116
Answer Key to Questions in Luke 167
Introduction to the Gospel of John 171
Study of John 172
Answer Key to Questions in John 238
Schedule of Bible Readings 243

Author's Note

Note: This study is designed to extend over thirteen weeks—one quarter of the calendar year. Each topic occupies one day. The study of the Gospel of Matthew runs for four weeks, Mark for two weeks, Luke lasts three weeks, and John continues for four weeks. Three or four simple study questions are intermingled with each day's reading. Please examine these as they arise in the reading. They will illuminate the topic of the preceding paragraph or in general aid your understanding the topic under discussion.

PREFACE

Scripture tells the reason for eternal life: "That they may know you, the only true God, and Jesus Christ whom you have sent" (John 17:3 NIV). You are about to begin a season of study in the first four books of the New Testament—Matthew, Mark, Luke, and John. These share the same wondrous subject: Jesus Christ whom God sent to live among us, full of grace and truth. May your study lead you into the full knowledge of him.

The gospels are a treasure store of information. Everything from weather forecasting to ethical precepts can be found here. Deeper than this, they hold the riches of God's truth. Believers find in these books spiritual principles for living a life of faith. Bible teachers find in them metaphors describing the church that formed after Jesus Christ completed his earthly ministry. The history and future of the faith may be found here.

These books follow on the heels of the Hebrew scriptures, which are commonly called the Old Testament. They were originally written to Jewish believers in Jesus Christ as records of the fulfillment of God's promises to their forefathers. The word *gospel* means "good news." For the people of ancient Israel, this good news focused on their Messiah who personifies the promises and fulfills the prophecies that overflow their scriptures. This study examines the four gospels from this point of view.

To fulfill these prophecies, Christ was sent only to the lost sheep of the house of Israel (Matthew 15:24). Still, the gospels contain precious instruction to those of us who do not hail from the tribes of Israel. They especially reveal the character and commission of the Son of God. However, the gospel of God's grace for the nations outside of Israel is not revealed in the gospels but in the writings of the apostle Paul.

While the four accounts of the Savior's life differ in many details, they reveal it with a similar plan. Each first introduces John the Baptist, who announces Christ's coming and the nearness of the kingdom of heaven. Then Christ begins his public ministry to Israel. When Israel rejects his ministry and its promised kingdom, Jesus privately ministers to his disciples until he is betrayed, crucified, and resurrected. These books contain the gospel of the kingdom, but this is limited to their earlier chapters. Before long, Israel refuses it. Then the kingdom is no longer preached, and the narrative focuses on the rejected Messiah and his descent to death on the cross.

The four accounts of our Lord's life have a common theme and a common plan. Yet, each bears a distinctive aspect of his glory. Opening words of each book give a general idea of its contents. Matthew 1:1 mentions the names of David and Abraham, presenting Israel's king and the inheritor of the Promised Land. Luke 3:38 casts back to Adam, presenting the suffering Son of Man. Mark 1:11 and John 1:14 present us with the Son of God. In Mark, he is seen in service to humanity. John reveals him in his ministry for God.

Do not take the readings of this book for anything more than suggestive thoughts on these essential topics. Allow them to do as they are intended—to lead you to the sacred scriptures. I would rather these thoughts disappear than stand between you and the divine revelation. So read each entry with a Bible at hand. Please examine face-to-face each scripture that is referenced and research each question. In this way, you allow the scripture to live and do as God would have it do—reveal Christ Jesus.

DANIEL PARTNER
Coos Bay, Oregon
December 15, 2004

INTRODUCTION TO THE
GOSPEL OF MATTHEW

In the first account of Jesus Christ's life, he wears the robes of royalty as the Son of David the king. A genealogy proves his claim to David's throne. Nobility surrounds his birth: The wise men acknowledge him as king of the Jews and because of this, King Herod tries to assassinate him. Then, in his ministry, Christ announces the kingdom to Israel, lays down its laws, and empowers his disciples to proclaim it.

Only Matthew uses the phrase *kingdom of the heavens*—a reference to the prophet Daniel: "The God of heaven will set up a kingdom that shall never be destroyed, nor shall this kingdom be left to another people. It shall crush all these kingdoms and bring them to an end, and it shall stand forever" (2:44). The primary significance of the parables in Matthew is in their revelation of this kingdom. The kingdom of the heavens, however, is not now in existence. It is the future earthly realm predicted by Daniel that will come after the overthrow of all earthly powers when voices in heaven proclaim, "The kingdoms of the world have become the kingdom of our Lord and of his Christ, and he will reign for ever and ever" (Revelation 15:11).

Matthew's narrative is divided into two distinct periods. Each opens with Christ's identification as the Son of God by a voice from heaven and closes with the same acknowledgment by a man. The first period extends from the Lord's baptism (3:16–17), and closes with Peter's confession, "You are the Christ, the Son of the living God" (16:16). During this period, the kingdom is offered and rejected. The second period concerns his preparation for sacrifice. It begins with the transformation on the mountain (17:1–5) and continues to the crucifixion and the centurion's confession, "Truly this was God's Son" (27:54).

Day One

Matthew 2:1–12

1 Now when Jesus was born in Bethlehem of Judaea in the days of Herod the king, behold, there came wise men from the east to Jerusalem,

2 Saying, Where is he that is born King of the Jews? for we have seen his star in the east, and are come to worship him.

3 When Herod the king had heard these things, he was troubled, and all Jerusalem with him.

4 And when he had gathered all the chief priests and scribes of the people together, he demanded of them where Christ should be born.

5 And they said unto him, In Bethlehem of Judaea: for thus it is written by the prophet,

6 And thou Bethlehem, in the land of Juda, art not the least among the princes of Juda: for out of thee shall come a Governor, that shall rule my people Israel.

7 Then Herod, when he had privily called the wise men, enquired of them diligently what time the star appeared.

8 And he sent them to Bethlehem, and said, Go and search diligently for the young child; and when ye have found him, bring me word again, that I may come and worship him also.

9 When they had heard the king, they departed; and, lo, the star, which they saw in the east, went before them, till it came and stood over where the young child was.

10 When they saw the star, they rejoiced with exceeding great joy.

11 And when they were come into the house, they saw the young child with Mary his mother, and fell down, and worshipped him: and when they had opened their treasures, they presented unto him gifts; gold, and frankincense and myrrh.

12 And being warned of God in a dream that they should not return to Herod, they departed into their own country another way.

Born in Bethlehem

The name *Bethlehem* means "house of bread." This little town is an apt birthplace for the man who is the Bread of Life (John 6:35). The town is connected with the family of Jesus Christ beginning at the time of the book of Ruth (c. 1375–1050 BC; Ruth 1:19). Still, Bethlehem is so insignificant that it is not even mentioned in the lists of the towns of Judah in Joshua 15 and Nehemiah 11.

1. Read Ruth 2:8 and compare it to Matthew 1:5. Which of Jesus' distant relatives lived in Bethlehem?

2. Read 1 Samuel 16:1, 11–13 and compare it to Matthew 1:6. Who else lived in Bethlehem who was one of Christ's forebears?

The three wise men appear every year in manger scenes and Christmas pageants. However, scripture does not say there were only three seekers from the east, but that they brought three types of gifts.

3. What were the three categories of the magi's gifts? (See Matthew 2:11.)

The magi represent those people who observe nature—people like outdoorsmen, scientists, and gardeners. Nature leads its pupils to the worship of its Creator.

Many attempts have been made to explain the star of Bethlehem as a purely normal occurrence. Could it be that the wise men followed a meteor, a comet, or the conjunction of a number of planets? But scientists can find no such celestial light during the time of the birth of Christ. Also, no such star could guide the magi for a long period and then take its place directly above Bethlehem. This was an extraordinary star, the like of which these stargazers from the east had never seen. It heralded the birth of a most extraordinary baby. This star teaches us that God will speak to seekers in a language they understand. For the wise men, it was the language of astronomy.

4. In Romans 1:20, what two aspects of God are revealed through the creation?

Day Two

Matthew 3:11–17

11 I indeed baptize you with water unto repentance. But he that cometh after me is mightier than I, whose shoes I am not worthy to bear: he shall baptize you with the Holy Ghost, and with fire:

12 Whose fan is in his hand, and he will throughly purge his floor, and gather his wheat into the garner; but he will burn up the chaff with unquenchable fire.

13 Then cometh Jesus from Galilee to Jordan unto John, to be baptized of him.

14 But John forbad him, saying, I have need to be baptized of thee, and comest thou to me?

15 And Jesus answering said unto him, Suffer it to be so now: for thus it becometh us to fulfil all righteousness. Then he suffered him.

16 And Jesus, when he was baptized, went up straightway out of the water: and, lo, the heavens were opened unto him, and he saw the Spirit of God descending like a dove, and lighting upon him:

17 And lo a voice from heaven, saying, This is my beloved Son, in whom I am well pleased.

The Descending Spirit

God's Spirit has no material form. So the scriptures depict it in various ways that suggest its force and significance. It is usually presented as a blast of air because this is the meaning of the Greek word *pneuma*, which is translated into English as "spirit."

1. How did Jesus describe the people who are born of the Spirit in John 3:8?

2. Read John 20:22. After the death and resurrection of Jesus, how did his disciples experience the Spirit?

In the time of Jesus' baptism, the Spirit is seen as a descending dove (Matthew 3:6). The significance of this image, though largely lost on us, would have moved a spiritual Israelite. The dove is usually considered an image of gentleness. So, the Lord advises his disciples to be as innocent as doves (10:16).

Here at his baptism there is an additional significance and deeper thought: Poor people in ancient Israel used doves for sacrifices. When Mary and Joseph presented Jesus to God at the temple, "They offered a sacrifice according to what is stated in the law of the Lord, 'a pair of turtledoves or two young pigeons.' " (Luke 2:24 NRSV). Jesus Christ is more than a gentle man. He is the sacrifice that anyone, rich or poor, can offer to God.

The Spirit of God invested Jesus Christ with power for the proclamation of the gospel of the kingdom. It did not present him with a warrior's sword and a king's scepter. It did not place him on a white horse or place a crown on his head. All this will come later. Rather, the Spirit of God supplied him with the far more godlike powers of gentleness, innocence, and sacrifice.

3. After the Lord ascended, his disciples embarked on their ministry. Read Acts 2:2. How did they experience the Spirit at that time?

DAY THREE

Matthew 4:12–17

12 Now when Jesus had heard that John was cast into prison, he departed into Galilee;

13 And leaving Nazareth, he came and dwelt in Capernaum, which is upon the sea coast, in the borders of Zabulon and Nephthalim:

14 That it might be fulfilled which was spoken by Esaias the prophet, saying,

15 The land of Zabulon, and the land of Nephthalim, by the way of the sea, beyond Jordan, Galilee of the Gentiles;

16 The people which sat in darkness saw great light; and to them which sat in the region and shadow of death light is sprung up.

17 From that time Jesus began to preach, and to say, Repent: for the kingdom of heaven is at hand.

The Gospel of the Kingdom

Jesus Christ preached the kingdom of the heavens. This meant only one thing to the Jews of those days. They recalled that the prophet Daniel explained the marvelous dream of King Nebuchadnezzar. Daniel 2:31–45 describes the huge statue that Nebuchadnezzar saw in his dream. The parts of this image represent the major world empires. God will set up the last of these kingdoms, which the Jews longed for.

1. Read Daniel 2:44. What does this kingdom do the all the previous kingdoms?

2. Isaiah 9:6 tells of Jesus Christ—the son that is born and the child that is given. What does verse 7 say about the length of his reign?

The *kingdom of God* is different from the *kingdom of the heavens.* In the kingdom of God, a person is a subject directly of God. In the coming kingdom of the heavens, Christ rules the earth through Israel. Furthermore, the kingdom of God has no boundaries; no borders. Presently, Christians are citizens of the kingdom of God. The kingdom of the heavens is specifically located on earth in the future with Jerusalem as its center. It is always concerned with the sovereignty of Israel over the nations of this world.

A Key to Nebuchadnezzar's dream:

• Babylon ruled the whole earth in Daniel's day. This is the gold head of the statue in the dream (Daniel 2:32). Babylon ruled the world from 625–539 BC.

• Medo-Persia succeeded Babylon and brought all nations beneath its sway (silver chest and arms; 539–331 BC).

• Alexander the Great overthrew the Persians and then found no field for further conquest (bronze middle and thighs; 331–164 BC).

• Rome followed the Greeks in world domination (v. 33; iron legs; 164 BC–AD 476).

• The feet of iron and clay represent the seven year rule of the anti-Christ in a future day.

3. In Romans 14:17, what are the three things that distinguish the kingdom of God?

Day Four

Matthew 5:38–48

38 Ye have heard that it hath been said, An eye for an eye, and a tooth for a tooth:

39 But I say unto you, That ye resist not evil: but whosoever shall smite thee on thy right cheek, turn to him the other also.

40 And if any man will sue thee at the law, and take away thy coat, let him have thy cloak also.

41 And whosoever shall compel thee to go a mile, go with him twain.

42 Give to him that asketh thee, and from him that would borrow of thee turn not thou away.

43 Ye have heard that it hath been said, Thou shalt love thy neighbour, and hate thine enemy.

44 But I say unto you, Love your enemies, bless them that curse you, do good to them that hate you, and pray for them which despitefully use you, and persecute you;

45 That ye may be the children of your Father which is in heaven: for he maketh his sun to rise on the evil and on the good, and sendeth rain on the just and on the unjust.

46 For if ye love them which love you, what reward have ye? do not even the publicans the same?

47 And if ye salute your brethren only, what do ye more than others? do not even the publicans so?

48 Be ye therefore perfect, even as your Father which is in heaven is perfect.

Be Imitators of God

Have you heard you should turn the other cheek if you are struck on the face? Have you actually done it? In Matthew 5:44, Jesus Christ says people should

• Love their enemies

• Bless the ones that curse them

- Do good to those that hate them

- Pray for people that despitefully use them

1. According to Matthew 5:45, how does Jesus persuade his audience to live as a child of the heavenly Father?

Most attempts to carry out Christ's principle of nonresistance are futile. Therefore, theologians recognize the practical difficulty of practicing the precepts of Matthew 5. They say that these expressions must not be taken literally. But, if we cannot take these sayings at face value, it is impossible to understand the Lord's reason for giving these instructions.

The key to understanding how this conduct is possible is to see its relation to the coming kingdom of the heavens. When the righteous king is on the throne such conduct will be not only right but also possible. This is ideal conduct for the time when the earth has an ideal government. This kingdom will be established after Christ comes again and Satan is bound for the thousand years (Revelation 20:1–3).

However, this does not release present-day believers from living in a way that expresses God. Therefore the apostle Paul urged the believers to "Be imitators of God, therefore, as dearly loved children and live a life of love, just as Christ loved us and gave himself up for us as a fragrant offering and sacrifice to God" (Ephesians 5:1–2 NRSV).

2. In Ephesians 5:1–2 how are we to live as imitators of God? (See verse 2.)

3. According to this verse, how does Paul persuade us to live in this way?

Day Five

Matthew 6:7–15

7 But when ye pray, use not vain repetitions, as the heathen do: for they think that they shall be heard for their much speaking.

8 Be not ye therefore like unto them: for your Father knoweth what things ye have need of, before ye ask him.

9 After this manner therefore pray ye: Our Father which art in heaven, Hallowed be thy name.

10 Thy kingdom come, Thy will be done in earth, as it is in heaven.

11 Give us this day our daily bread.

12 And forgive us our debts, as we forgive our debtors.

13 And lead us not into temptation, but deliver us from evil: For thine is the kingdom, and the power, and the glory, for ever. Amen.

14 For if ye forgive men their trespasses, your heavenly Father will also forgive you:

15 But if ye forgive not men their trespasses, neither will your Father forgive your trespasses.

The Model Prayer

Matthew 6:9–13 is not actually the Lord's Prayer, as it is now called. Rather, it is Christ's model for the disciples' prayers. Jesus condemned wordiness in prayer (v. 7). So, he gives his disciples this example of how to say much with few words. Therefore, this example of prayer should not become a text for endless repetition.

This pattern of prayer is exquisitely formed around seven petitions. Three express God's glory and four express humanity's needs.

1. In Matthew 6:9–10, what are the petitions that express God's glory?

2. In verses 11–13, what four petitions express humanity's needs?

Every petition in this prayer will be fulfilled when the kingdom has come. Then Christ's followers will be safe from the wicked one because Satan will be bound in the pit (Revelation 20:2–3). Then their trials are over, their debts paid, and their daily nourishment assured. Then God's will is done on earth and his name hallowed by a holy nation.

The best prayers for this age of grace are found in Ephesians (1:17–23; 3:14–21). These are concerned with the outpouring of grace (Ephesians 3:8). It was Paul's unique commission to make everyone see the plan of this mystery (v. 9). This is why he prays, "that, according to the riches of his glory, he may grant that you may be strengthened in your inner being with power through his Spirit" (Ephesians 3:16). Notice, this is not a prayer for spiritual power to serve God or perform miracles. Paul certainly does not pray for strength enough to get through the day. Great power is required to enable us to realize and appreciate the marvelous revelation of God's grace and love that is ours in Christ Jesus. May God exercise our hearts to this end!

3. Compare Matthew 6:12 with Ephesians 1:7. In which of these verses is forgiveness conditional?

Day Six

Matthew 6:25–34

25 Therefore I say unto you, Take no thought for your life, what ye shall eat, or what ye shall drink; nor yet for your body, what ye shall put on. Is not the life more than meat, and the body than raiment?

26 Behold the fowls of the air: for they sow not, neither do they reap, nor gather into barns; yet your heavenly Father feedeth them. Are ye not much better than they?

27 Which of you by taking thought can add one cubit unto his stature?

28 And why take ye thought for raiment? Consider the lilies of the field, how they grow; they toil not, neither do they spin:

29 And yet I say unto you, That even Solomon in all his glory was not arrayed like one of these.

30 Wherefore, if God so clothe the grass of the field, which to day is, and to morrow is cast into the oven, shall he not much more clothe you, O ye of little faith?

31 Therefore take no thought, saying, What shall we eat? or, What shall we drink? or, Wherewithal shall we be clothed?

32 (For after all these things do the Gentiles seek:) for your heavenly Father knoweth that ye have need of all these things.

33 But seek ye first the kingdom of God, and his righteousness; and all these things shall be added unto you.

34 Take therefore no thought for the morrow: for the morrow shall take thought for the things of itself. Sufficient unto the day is the evil thereof.

The Scriptural Relief for Worry

Humankind has become the slave of physical desire. Instead of eating and drinking to live, lives are spent laboring just to be able to eat and drink. In contrast, plants and animals display of God's continual care and provision.

The scriptures show a progression in the experience of believers in relationship to worry. This changes as God's grace becomes more fully known:

1. Read what the Psalmist sang in Psalm 55:22. What is his solution to worry?

2. In the encouraging words of Matthew 6:25–34, relief is conditional. In verse 33, what is that condition?

Worry is a killer. Philippians 6:6–7 gives the secret of how to get beyond its reach. It tells of one of the most precious privileges of all who are in Christ—prayer: "Do not be anxious about anything, but in everything, by prayer and petition, with thanksgiving, present your requests to God. And the peace of God, which transcends all understanding, will guard your hearts and your minds in Christ Jesus" (NIV).

These verses do not promise that our prayers will be answered. They go far deeper than that. God is guiding all things to the divine goal and is not hindered by the worries that distress us. When we present our requests to God through prayer and petition with thanksgiving, we agree with God's will no matter if our prayers are answered. Then we enter into an inexplicable peace that guards our hearts and minds from further worries. This is difficult to explain—but we can experience it through prayer.

3. Peter 5:7 was written to the dispersed Jewish believers. How is the burden of worry relieved in this verse?

4. What is the replacement for worry in Philippians 4:6–7?

Day Seven

Matthew 7:15–23

15 Beware of false prophets, which come to you in sheep's clothing, but inwardly they are ravening wolves.

16 Ye shall know them by their fruits. Do men gather grapes of thorns, or figs of thistles?

17 Even so every good tree bringeth forth good fruit; but a corrupt tree bringeth forth evil fruit.

18 A good tree cannot bring forth evil fruit, neither can a corrupt tree bring forth good fruit.

19 Every tree that bringeth not forth good fruit is hewn down, and cast into the fire.

20 Wherefore by their fruits ye shall know them.

21 Not every one that saith unto me, Lord, Lord, shall enter into the kingdom of heaven; but he that doeth the will of my Father which is in heaven.

22 Many will say to me in that day, Lord, Lord, have we not prophesied in thy name? and in thy name have cast out devils? and in thy name done many wonderful works?

23 And then will I profess unto them, I never knew you: depart from me, ye that work iniquity.

True and False Prophets

Jesus Christ dismantles the common idea that anyone who can prophesy, cast out demons, or do other supernatural deeds is intimate with God. Matthew 7:22–23 says many will claim these powers, yet Christ refuses to recognize them. Supernatural occurrences do not necessarily indicate divine activity. In fact, the powers of evil can triumph while mimicking the manifestations of the Holy Spirit (2 Corinthians 11:14).

Christ's words of Matthew 7:16—"Ye shall know them by their fruits. Do men gather grapes of thorns, or figs of thistles?"—are spoken in the light of Micah 4:4—"But they shall sit every man under his vine and under his fig tree."

The fig tree stands for the righteous government of the Messiah and the vine the spiritual cheer of his kingdom. In that day, each one will sit under his personal vine and fig tree. This is not to say that today the kingdom of God is simply a matter of feeding on figs and drinking wine. Today, these symbolize righteousness, peace, and joy in the Holy Spirit (Romans 14:17). Such spiritual fruits characterize the true prophet and do not grow on thorns and thistles.

The Jewish law was especially hard on false prophets:

1. Read Deuteronomy 13:5. What is the penalty for a false prophet?

2. Read verses 1–3. Why would God allow a false prophecy to come true?

The term *prophet* includes those who claim a direct revelation from God apart from the Bible's written revelation. Like Israel, the church has true prophets. Men like Peter and Paul functioned at the inception of the church. However, since their generation passed from the scene the mere claim to a personal and direct message from God is evidence that it is false.

3. Read Ephesians 2:20. Where are the prophets located in the church?

The word of God is complete (Colossians 1:25). The revelations given to the apostle Paul make all further prophecy useless. Only those people who do not understand what God has revealed hunger after more divine communiqués.

DAY EIGHT

Matthew 8:14–22

14 And when Jesus was come into Peter's house, he saw his wife's mother laid, and sick of a fever.

15 And he touched her hand, and the fever left her: and she arose, and ministered unto them.

16 When the even was come, they brought unto him many that were possessed with devils: and he cast out the spirits with his word, and healed all that were sick:

17 That it might be fulfilled which was spoken by Esaias the prophet, saying, Himself took our infirmities, and bare our sicknesses.

18 Now when Jesus saw great multitudes about him, he gave commandment to depart unto the other side.

19 And a certain scribe came, and said unto him, Master, I will follow thee whithersoever thou goest.

20 And Jesus saith unto him, The foxes have holes, and the birds of the air have nests; but the Son of man hath not where to lay his head.

21 And another of his disciples said unto him, Lord, suffer me first to go and bury my father.

22 But Jesus said unto him, Follow me; and let the dead bury their dead.

The Son of Man

In Matthew 8:16, Jesus displays the kingdom's power by casting out demons and healing all who came to him. Multitudes of people, full of demands, surround him.

1. Read Matthew 8:19. What does the religious scribe call Jesus? What does Jesus call himself in 8:20?

The title *Son of Man* shows that Christ is capable of coping with all that Adam's sin has brought into the world. He has regained the sovereignty lost by that first man. The kingdom he offers to Israel extends over all mankind, over the beasts of the field, and the birds of the air. But here, a scribe thinks that Jesus Christ is only a teacher (Matthew 8:19). This shows that Israel has no idea that he is the Messiah of the promised kingdom. So, the jackals can rest in their burrows, the birds have roosts on which to spend the night, yet the weary head of the man whose kingdom includes all earthly creatures has nowhere to recline and sleep (v. 20).

2. In 1 Corinthians 15:45, what is Adam? What is Christ?

3. In Matthew 8, Christ has nowhere to rest his head. What is the difference between Christ's head in Matthew 27:29 and in Revelation 14:14?

The title *Son of Man* (Matthew 8:20) is significant in every place it occurs in scripture. It indicates the dignities that were entrusted to Adam as the ruler of all earthly creatures and head of the human race. Jesus Christ inherited all these glories and will restore them in the coming kingdom age.

4. Read 1 Corinthians 15:47. What image do we bear today? What image will we bear in the future?

Day Nine

Matthew 9:27–34

27 And when Jesus departed thence, two blind men followed him, crying, and saying, Thou son of David, have mercy on us.

28 And when he was come into the house, the blind men came to him: and Jesus saith unto them, Believe ye that I am able to do this? They said unto him, Yea, Lord.

29 Then touched he their eyes, saying, According to your faith be it unto you.

30 And their eyes were opened; and Jesus straitly charged them, saying, See that no man know it.

31 But they, when they were departed, spread abroad his fame in all that country.

32 As they went out, behold, they brought to him a dumb man possessed with a devil.

33 And when the devil was cast out, the dumb spake: and the multitudes marvelled, saying, It was never so seen in Israel.

34 But the Pharisees said, He casteth out devils through the prince of the devils.

Christ's Power Over Satan

One of the chief features of the kingdom of the heavens will be the absence of Satan and other evil spirits. At the end of this age, in preparation for the kingdom, the wild beast is arrested (19:20), and the dragon is bound for the thousand years (20:2). So, when Jesus casts out demons, he demonstrates his power to take the kingdom's throne. His power over the unseen domains of darkness is proof that he is the Messiah.

1. Read Revelation 13:2. Who gives the beast his power, throne, and authority?

Jesus Christ demonstrated the powers of the coming kingdom age in his healing and casting out of demons. The purpose of these demonstrations was to convince Israel that their Messiah had come and persuade the nation to believe in him. The Pharisees said Jesus' miraculous signs indicated not that he was the Messiah but that he was in league with the powers of darkness. Therefore, it was impossible for them or their followers to repent and believe. The Pharisees committed the unpardonable sin when they credited the work of God's Holy Spirit to Satan.

2. In Matthew 9:34, who did the Pharisees say gave Jesus his Messianic powers?

3. Matthew 12:31–32 gives a name to this statement. What is it? (See verse 31.)

Today we face the opposite danger of crediting all supernatural manifestations to the Holy Spirit. This is why Paul warned, "The Spirit clearly says that in later times some will abandon the faith and follow deceiving spirits and things taught by demons" (1 Timothy 4:1 NIV); and John advised, "Dear friends, do not believe every spirit, but test the spirits to see whether they are from God" (1 John 4:1 NIV).

Character Study—Matthew
And as Jesus passed forth from thence, he saw a man, named Matthew, sitting at the receipt of custom: and he saith unto him, Follow me. And he arose, and followed him (Matthew 9:9).

The fact that such a man as Matthew should be chosen for an apostle is a striking exhibition of God's grace and wisdom. Not only so, the fact that this man was empowered to write this account of Israel's king was contrary to human wisdom (1 Corinthians 2:13).

Matthew was a publican, a tax collector. He belonged to a class more hated in Israel than foreigners and more despised than sinners. The Roman government did not directly collect its taxes from the nations it ruled. This task was farmed out to contractors—the publicans. A district was sold to a publican for what it would bring to the government in taxes. The tax collector, in this case, Matthew, made his money by assessing as much as he could get above the official tax rate. Hence, he amassed wealth at the expense of his countrymen and for the benefit of a foreign government. Yet, God chose Matthew, a traitor to his country, not only as an apostle but also to describe in writing the glories of the heavenly king. Matthew's fitness for this task was not his by birth or by approval of his fellowmen, but given by God in grace (Ephesians 2:8–9).

Day Ten

Matthew 10:1–15

1 And when he had called unto him his twelve disciples, he gave them power against unclean spirits, to cast them out, and to heal all manner of sickness and all manner of disease.

2 Now the names of the twelve apostles are these; The first, Simon, who is called Peter, and Andrew his brother; James the son of Zebedee, and John his brother;

3 Philip, and Bartholomew; Thomas, and Matthew the publican; James the son of Alphaeus, and Lebbaeus, whose surname was Thaddaeus;

4 Simon the Canaanite, and Judas Iscariot, who also betrayed him.

5 These twelve Jesus sent forth, and commanded them, saying, Go not into the way of the Gentiles, and into any city of the Samaritans enter ye not:

6 But go rather to the lost sheep of the house of Israel.

7 And as ye go, preach, saying, The kingdom of heaven is at hand.

8 Heal the sick, cleanse the lepers, raise the dead, cast out devils: freely ye have received, freely give.

9 Provide neither gold, nor silver, nor brass in your purses,

10 Nor scrip for your journey, neither two coats, neither shoes, nor yet staves: for the workman is worthy of his meat.

11 And into whatsoever city or town ye shall enter, enquire who in it is worthy; and there abide till ye go thence.

12 And when ye come into an house, salute it.

13 And if the house be worthy, let your peace come upon it: but if it be not worthy, let your peace return to you.

14 And whosoever shall not receive you, nor hear your words, when ye depart out of that house or city, shake off the dust of your feet.

15 Verily I say unto you, It shall be more tolerable for the land of Sodom and Gomorrha in the day of judgment, than for that city.

The Progress of the Preaching of the Kingdom

Up to this time, Jesus had been heralding the kingdom alone, establishing the message with miraculous signs that indicated its nearness. Now, he associates himself and his work with twelve of his disciples and sends them out to Israel with authority over disease, death, and the demons. In this way, they, too, could prove the kingdom's nearness by their words and their works. However, they were only to go to Israel. Not even nearby Samaria was to hear the kingdom message (Matthew 10:5). It was strictly for the lost sheep of Israel's fold.

1. In Matthew 28:16–20, Jesus sends the disciples out a second time with the kingdom message. Who is this message for? What nation is not included in his instructions?

The first kingdom proclamation carried on until it was clear that Israel had rejected Jesus and his message. At that time, he instructed his disciples that they should tell no one that he was the Messiah (16:20). The proclamation of the kingdom of the heavens was interrupted from this time until the day of Pentecost.

2. Matthew 17:9 specifies the time the disciples can again tell of the Messiah and his kingdom. When is this?

Peter sees that Jesus is the Messiah, the Son of the living God (16:15–17). Still, for the latter half of the book of Matthew the door to the kingdom remains locked and its proclamation forbidden. The preaching of the kingdom will begin again after Christ's ascension. This is why Jesus gives the keys of the kingdom to Peter (16:19). At Pentecost, Peter uses these keys to unlock the kingdom again.

3. Read Acts 2:37–39. What are the conditions for the entrance of Israel into the kingdom?

A small percentage of the people accept the kingdom message of Peter and the eleven. Soon Stephen and James are murdered (7:58–60; 12:1–2) and attempts are made on the lives of Peter and Paul (12:3; 9:23). Thus, Israel again rejects the kingdom of the heavens. At the end of Acts, it is formally set aside by Paul's public announcement of the nation's apostasy (28:23–28).

4. When Paul locks Israel out of the kingdom in Acts 28:23–28, whom does he say will then listen to the gospel?

God will again turn to Israel in the future, and the kingdom will once more be proclaimed. In the midst of great affliction, the nation, represented by the hundred and forty-four thousand (Revelation 7:3–8) and the great multitude (7:9–17), will accept the proclamation and enter the kingdom. Then Peter's epistles will unlock the kingdom's door for those of the Jewish race, and all Israel will be saved (Romans 11:26). The kingdom will be present on the earth, and there will be no more need of its proclamation.

Christ's gospel of the kingdom is not concerned with sin or individual salvation. The pardon of sins, based on the sufferings of Christ, is seen in Luke's account of Jesus Christ's commission for mankind (Luke 24:46–49) and is not confined to Israel. Here in Matthew, when the gospel of the kingdom was first proclaimed, Christ had not yet suffered, so his preaching referred only to the kingdom promised to Israel in the Old Testament.

DAY ELEVEN

Matthew 11:1–15

1 And it came to pass, when Jesus had made an end of commanding his twelve disciples, he departed thence to teach and to preach in their cities.

2 Now when John had heard in the prison the works of Christ, he sent two of his disciples,

3 And said unto him, Art thou he that should come, or do we look for another?

4 Jesus answered and said unto them, Go and shew John again those things which ye do hear and see:

5 The blind receive their sight, and the lame walk, the lepers are cleansed, and the deaf hear, the dead are raised up, and the poor have the gospel preached to them.

6 And blessed is he, whosoever shall not be offended in me.

7 And as they departed, Jesus began to say unto the multitudes concerning John, What went ye out into the wilderness to see? A reed shaken with the wind?

8 But what went ye out for to see? A man clothed in soft raiment? behold, they that wear soft clothing are in kings' houses.

9 But what went ye out for to see? A prophet? yea, I say unto you, and more than a prophet.

10 For this is he, of whom it is written, Behold, I send my messenger before thy face, which shall prepare thy way before thee.

11 Verily I say unto you, Among them that are born of women there hath not risen a greater than John the Baptist: notwithstanding he that is least in the kingdom of heaven is greater than he.

12 And from the days of John the Baptist until now the kingdom of heaven suffereth violence, and the violent take it by force.

13 For all the prophets and the law prophesied until John.

14 And if ye will receive it, this is Elias, which was for to come.

15 He that hath ears to hear, let him hear.

John the Baptist

John was the greatest of all the prophets (Matthew 11:11). Yet, even he is not fully aware of the mind of God. So, he wonders, *If Christ is the Messiah, why am I allowed to languish in prison?* (See Matthew 11:2–3.)

1. King Herod put John in prison. Why? (Read Matthew 14:3–4.)

In those days, the Jews had difficulty reconciling the prophecies of the Messiah. Some saw him as the suffering one; others made him a glorious king. Still others looked for two messiahs: one, a man to suffer, and another a king to reign.

John the Baptist had openly rebuked Herod and so had been imprisoned (Matthew 14:3). Jesus made no effort to get him out of Herod's hands and did nothing to claim messianic power. John may have begun to consider the option of two Messiahs. Was Jesus the suffering one, and was there to be another to rule with an iron rod? We now see that Jesus embodied a combination of suffering and glory with an interval between the two. He suffered on the cross, and he will come again to rule in his kingdom. This was not clear to John or anyone else in his era.

2. Compare Matthew 11:14 with Malachi 4:4–5. Who is Malachi prophesying about?

Yes, John asks a question of the Lord, but this does not mean that he is a weakling or lover of luxury. He is not wavering in his confidence in Christ or looking for his own comfort (Matthew 11:8). People came out to see a true prophet, and that was what they saw (v. 9). His imprisonment is an added proof of this. It is the usual reward for a man of God (Jeremiah 37:16–17). Here, the Lord gives John a eulogy that places him on the highest pinnacle of human fame with a name greater than Moses and Elijah (vv. 13–14).

3. Read Matthew 11:13. What ended the speaking of the Old Testament Law and Prophets?

DAY TWELVE

Matthew 11:20–28

20 Then began he to upbraid the cities wherein most of his mighty works were done, because they repented not:

21 Woe unto thee, Chorazin! woe unto thee, Bethsaida! for if the mighty works, which were done in you, had been done in Tyre and Sidon, they would have repented long ago in sackcloth and ashes.

22 But I say unto you, It shall be more tolerable for Tyre and Sidon at the day of judgment, than for you.

23 And thou, Capernaum, which art exalted unto heaven, shalt be brought down to hell: for if the mighty works, which have been done in thee, had been done in Sodom, it would have remained until this day.

24 But I say unto you, That it shall be more tolerable for the land of Sodom in the day of judgment, than for thee.

25 At that time Jesus answered and said, I thank thee, O Father, Lord of heaven and earth, because thou hast hid these things from the wise and prudent, and hast revealed them unto babes.

26 Even so, Father: for so it seemed good in thy sight.

27 All things are delivered unto me of my Father: and no man knoweth the Son, but the Father; neither knoweth any man the Father, save the Son, and he to whomsoever the Son will reveal him.

28 Come unto me, all ye that labour and are heavy laden, and I will give you rest.

The Light Yoke of Failure

Though his ministry seems to be a failure, Jesus says, "Yes, Father for such was your gracious will" (Matthew 11:26 NRSV), recognizing the fact that this apparent failure is in accord with God's purpose. He agrees with God's delight in hiding the truth from those who are wise and intelligent in the things of this life. He cannot reach them with the gospel of the kingdom. God's work is apparently without the anticipated results. Yet Jesus knows that, in the final analysis, God is operating all things for his own purpose and glory.

1. Why did Jesus reproach the cities of Chorazin and Beth-saida? (Read Matthew 11:20.)

2. In Matthew 11:25, why do the wise and intelligent people not see the things of God?

Jesus' invitation, "Come unto me, all you that are weary and are carrying heavy burdens, and I will give you rest" (v. 28) is given new meaning in light of his recognition of God's hand in all things for the fulfillment of the divine plan. This gives the hearts of his followers ease and their spirits rest. This is especially true in days of apostasy such as confronted the disciples.

The thought that failure is not of God and that success is his hallmark is false. Christ's own ministry is our prime example of this. Today however, disobedience to God's will is fully justified if it results in apparent success. It is hard for pride to be involved in failure. Why not throw off the yoke of God's will and ensure success by human methods? The reason is because that is a heavy yoke to bear. Christ's mind is to bow humbly beneath the failure that is according to God's purpose. We please God by suffering rejection along with him.

3. The apostle Paul portrays the Lord's light yoke. How does he describe this in Philippians 2:5?

DAY THIRTEEN

Matthew 13:1–12

1 The same day went Jesus out of the house, and sat by the sea side.

2 And great multitudes were gathered together unto him, so that he went into a ship, and sat; and the whole multitude stood on the shore.

3 And he spake many things unto them in parables, saying, Behold, a sower went forth to sow;

4 And when he sowed, some seeds fell by the way side, and the fowls came and devoured them up:

5 Some fell upon stony places, where they had not much earth: and forthwith they sprung up, because they had no deepness of earth:

6 And when the sun was up, they were scorched; and because they had no root, they withered away.

7 And some fell among thorns; and the thorns sprung up, and choked them:

8 But other fell into good ground, and brought forth fruit, some an hundredfold, some sixtyfold, some thirtyfold.

9 Who hath ears to hear, let him hear.

10 And the disciples came, and said unto him, Why speakest thou unto them in parables?

11 He answered and said unto them, Because it is given unto you to know the mysteries of the kingdom of heaven, but to them it is not given.

12 For whosoever hath, to him shall be given, and he shall have more abundance: but whosoever hath not, from him shall be taken away even that he hath.

Sowing the Seeds of the Kingdom

The gospel of the kingdom has been rejected. So Jesus does two things: He repudiates his relatives (Matthew 12:46–50)—his connection in the flesh with the nation of Israel—and he goes out of the house to sit beside the sea (13:1). In other words, he takes himself outside the Jewish system.

Vast throngs come to him there. But he no longer proclaims the nearness of the kingdom. Instead, he speaks so they cannot understand, concealing his meaning in parables. His subject is still the kingdom, but his approach is different. He speaks of secrets that even his disciples cannot understand.

By comparing the kingdom with the sowing, growing, and harvesting of a crop, Jesus indicates that it has been removed to a distance in time. A field of wheat takes time to grow. Had the kingdom still been just around the corner, he would not have called himself a sower, but a reaper—a harvester.

1. Read Matthew 3:2 and 4:17. Who sows the seeds of the kingdom of the heavens?

2. In Revelation 14:14–16, who reaps the harvest of the kingdom?

This parable shows us why Christ's message did not sweep Israel into the kingdom. In those days, unfenced fields were allotted to farmers and the roads ran right through the growing grain. It was impossible for the farmers to avoid broadcasting some seed on the hard ground. There were certainly outcroppings of rock and shallow soil in and near the fields. Thorny weeds were thick and difficult to eradicate.

The people of Israel were much like their farmers' fields. It takes the sun and rain of heaven to change rocks into fertile soil. As Jesus spoke, the hearts of the people of Israel were still hard. It will take the storms of persecution and the fire of affliction to prepare them for the kingdom of Christ (Matthew 24:21–22).

3. Romans 10:10 tells what we use to believe and be justified by God. What is it we use for this purpose?

We Gentile believers must also be concerned with the condition of our hearts. God sent the Spirit of his Son into our hearts (Galatians 4:6). The apostle prays, as should we, that the eyes of our hearts be enlightened (Ephesians 1:17). And we are exhorted to let the peace of Christ rule in our hearts (Colossians 3:15). Surely, the parable of the sower, though addressed to Israel, holds a lesson for us as well.

In light of the parable of the sower, each believer might benefit by praying, *God my Father, establish my heart to be without blame in holiness before you at the coming of the Lord Jesus Christ with all his holy ones* (1 Thessalonians 3:13).

DAY FOURTEEN

Matthew 13:36–45

36 Then Jesus sent the multitude away, and went into the house: and his disciples came unto him, saying, Declare unto us the parable of the tares of the field.

37 He answered and said unto them, He that soweth the good seed is the Son of man;

38 The field is the world; the good seed are the children of the kingdom; but the tares are the children of the wicked one;

39 The enemy that sowed them is the devil; the harvest is the end of the world; and the reapers are the angels.

40 As therefore the tares are gathered and burned in the fire; so shall it be in the end of this world.

41 The Son of man shall send forth his angels, and they shall gather out of his kingdom all things that offend, and them which do iniquity;

42 And shall cast them into a furnace of fire: there shall be wailing and gnashing of teeth.

43 Then shall the righteous shine forth as the sun in the kingdom of their Father. Who hath ears to hear, let him hear.

44 Again, the kingdom of heaven is like unto treasure hid in a field; the which when a man hath found, he hideth, and for joy thereof goeth and selleth all that he hath, and buyeth that field.

45 Again, the kingdom of heaven is like unto a merchant man, seeking goodly pearls:

The Treasure in the Field

Israel as a country has often been subject to conflict—revolutions, raids, and invasions. Therefore, in the ancient days, it was customary to hide money and valuables in secret vaults in the fields. It would be dangerous to dig in another man's field, so in the parable of the treasure hidden in the field, the field must be purchased.

1. Read Matthew 13:38. What does the field represent in this parable?

Israel is the treasure in the field. To possess the treasure, the Son of Man gives all he has to purchase the world. We who believe know that he has paid its price with his life.

The parable of the pearl is another aspect of the truth that is revealed by the parable of the treasure hidden in the field. Pearls grow in the sea. The sea represents the nations of this world among whom Israel is scattered (Revelation 17:5). The chosen nation dispersed among the nations is the precious pearl sought by the merchant. This man represents the Son of Man who gave up all his riches to purchase that pearl. They will be his special treasure in the day of the coming kingdom.

Some say that Christ is the pearl that is found by a sinner seeking salvation.

2. Romans 3:11 tells who seeks God. Who is this?

3. The scripture tells who is the seeker. Read Luke 15:6, 9, 24; 19:10 to find out who this is.

Others say that the church is that which is hidden in the field or is the pearl of great price. The church, however, is not in view at this time. Jesus is ministering to Israel. Matthew likens the pearl and the treasure to the kingdom of the heavens (Matthew 13:44–45). This kingdom belongs to Israel and her Messiah.

It is true, Christ gave himself for the church (Ephesians 5:25). This is because Christ and the church are one body (Ephesians 1:22–23). Christ's motive is entirely different from that of the merchant in Matthew 13:45. The church is not separate from Christ like the pearl is from the merchant. A husband is exhorted to love his wife as his own body because in this way Christ loves the church. They are not separate.

Day Fifteen

Matthew 15:21–28

21 Then Jesus went thence, and departed into the coasts of Tyre and Sidon.

22 And, behold, a woman of Canaan came out of the same coasts, and cried unto him, saying, Have mercy on me, O Lord, thou son of David; my daughter is grievously vexed with a devil.

23 But he answered her not a word. And his disciples came and besought him, saying, Send her away; for she crieth after us.

24 But he answered and said, I am not sent but unto the lost sheep of the house of Israel.

25 Then came she and worshipped him, saying, Lord, help me.

26 But he answered and said, It is not meet to take the children's bread, and to cast it to dogs.

27 And she said, Truth, Lord: yet the dogs eat of the crumbs which fall from their masters' table.

28 Then Jesus answered and said unto her, O woman, great is thy faith: be it unto thee even as thou wilt. And her daughter was made whole from that very hour.

Crumbs Under Israel's Table

The incident of the Canaanite woman is of special interest because it shows the status of the non-Jewish nations in Christ's earthly ministry. People of these nations are commonly called Gentiles.

This foreign woman knows that Jesus is the Son of David, king of Israel (Matthew 15:22). Still, she begs his help in healing her daughter. In her desperation, she ignores the fact that he is Israel's king. So, Jesus answers not a word. It would be a mistake to suppose that he does not wish to be gracious to the woman. She is simply knocking on the wrong door.

1. Compare Matthew 15:22 with 15:25. What is the difference between these two verses regarding the way the Canaanite woman addressed Jesus?

This woman first addressed the Son of David—the son of Israel's great king. A king is like a father of his people. They are his children to whom he supplies all things. But this woman is a Canaanite and has no claim on his blessings. This is the key to understanding Christ's earthly ministry.

2. In Romans 15:8, whom does Jesus Christ serve?

3. Ephesians 2:12 describes the two features of the Canaanite woman's position in relation to Israel. What are these two features?

Contrasts between the ministries of Christ and Paul:

• Christ was the servant of the circumcision (Romans 15:8). Paul was a minister for the nations (2 Timothy 1:11).

• Christ "became a servant of the circumcised on behalf of the truth of God [to] confirm the promises made to the patriarchs" (Romans 15:8 NRSV). Paul was a "minister of Christ Jesus to the Gentiles in the priestly service of the gospel of God" (v.16).

• Christ never went outside the land of Israel. Paul was not called until he had left the land of Israel (Acts 9:3–6).

• Christ was sent only to the lost sheep of the house of Israel (Matthew 15:24). Jesus Christ sent Paul to the Gentiles (Acts 9:15).

Throughout the Lord's public life, he stressed that his mission was exclusively to Israel. So, the Canaanite woman had to take the place of an outcast before she could get a crumb from Israel's table.

Christ is Lord of all (Acts 10:36). Under this title, the Canaanite woman is within his jurisdiction. So, she calls out for help addressing Jesus as Lord (Matthew 15:25). Still, she is not equal to an Israelite. Only the scraps of Israel's blessings are for her. Had we lived in the time of Christ, we Gentiles would have had this place in his ministry. It was not until Paul's letter to the Ephesians that it is seen that we have been brought near and entered the family of God (Ephesians 2:18–19).

The progress of the Gentiles into God's blessings:

- Matthew 10:5–6—The twelve apostles are told, "Go nowhere among the Gentiles."
- Acts10:1–48—The apostles learn that Gentile converts to Judaism can share Israel's blessings.
- Acts 13:46–47—Paul opens the door to Gentiles who are not converts.
- Acts 28:29—The salvation of God is sent directly to the nations.

In the present administration of God's grace, the nations are no longer inferior to Israel as they were in the Gospels and the apostle Paul's earlier ministry. This is seen in Ephesians 2:11–22.

4. Romans 9:4–5 lists the eight items of Israel's unique blessing. What are these items?

DAY SIXTEEN

Matthew 16:13–20

13 When Jesus came into the coasts of Caesarea Philippi, he asked his disciples, saying, Whom do men say that I the Son of man am?

14 And they said, Some say that thou art John the Baptist: some, Elias; and others, Jeremias, or one of the prophets.

15 He saith unto them, But whom say ye that I am?

16 And Simon Peter answered and said, Thou art the Christ, the Son of the living God.

17 And Jesus answered and said unto him, Blessed art thou, Simon Barjona: for flesh and blood hath not revealed it unto thee, but my Father which is in heaven.

18 And I say also unto thee, That thou art Peter, and upon this rock I will build my church; and the gates of hell shall not prevail against it.

19 And I will give unto thee the keys of the kingdom of heaven: and whatsoever thou shalt bind on earth shall be bound in heaven: and whatsoever thou shalt loose on earth shall be loosed in heaven.

20 Then charged he his disciples that they should tell no man that he was Jesus the Christ.

The Revelation of the Christ

Here is the climax of Jesus Christ's proclamation of the kingdom. By this time, no one among the people of Israel knows who he is. The few gathered here, led by Peter, recognize Jesus as Israel's Messiah. They constitute the new church. They have been called out from the nation, separated by loyalty to the Christ.

The meaning of the name *Peter* is "rock." Jesus plays on this meaning, saying, "On this rock I will build my church" (Matthew 16:18 NRSV). In other words, this group of called-out Israelites, this church, would be built on Peter and his revelation of Christ. Only he is the foundation in this church because he alone first understands that Jesus is the Christ, Israel's Messiah.

1. Read Revelation 21:14. Upon whom is the New Jerusalem built?

After Peter's confession in Caesarea Philippi, the doors into the kingdom were shut and Jesus no longer proclaimed it. The Lord would not be present when the kingdom's doors opened again. So, he gave Peter the keys (v. 19), which he later used to reopen the kingdom of the heavens.

2. Peter used the keys to the kingdom in Acts 2:38. What are these two keys?

3. Read Galatians 2:8. Who is the apostle to the circumcision (the Jews)? Who is the apostle to the Gentiles?

Peter's dealings with Ananias and Sapphira show the remarkable power he possessed when the kingdom of the heavens was again proclaimed in Israel (5:1–11). However, none of this has any connection with the present church, the body of Christ. We are not built on Peter, the apostle to the circumcision (Galatians 2:8), and his teaching is not directly for us. We are primarily associated with Paul, the apostle to the nations.

Day Seventeen

Matthew 17:1–8

1 And after six days Jesus taketh Peter, James, and John his brother, and bringeth them up into an high mountain apart,

2 And was transfigured before them: and his face did shine as the sun, and his raiment was white as the light.

3 And, behold, there appeared unto them Moses and Elias talking with him.

4 Then answered Peter, and said unto Jesus, Lord, it is good for us to be here: if thou wilt, let us make here three tabernacles; one for thee, and one for Moses, and one for Elias.

5 While he yet spake, behold, a bright cloud overshadowed them: and behold a voice out of the cloud, which said, This is my beloved Son, in whom I am well pleased; hear ye him.

6 And when the disciples heard it, they fell on their face, and were sore afraid.

7 And Jesus came and touched them, and said, Arise, and be not afraid.

8 And when they had lifted up their eyes, they saw no man, save Jesus only.

Listen to the Beloved Son

The event on the mountain recorded in Matthew 17 is commonly called the Transfiguration. But this is not merely a transfiguration but a transformation. The difference is significant.

At present, Satan is transfigured into a messenger of light (2 Corinthians 11:14). Conversely, we should be transformed by the renewing of our minds (Romans 12:2). Transfiguration is a temporary change of fashion. Satan's actual nature is much darker than that of an angel of light. Transformation, however, reveals one's actual appearance. Our transformation in the spirit of our mind is not a temporary change.

The Lord's flesh was a veil or curtain that hid his inherent splendor. Here on the mountain, his glory shines out so that it becomes visible to mortal eyes. He is transformed into his actual appearance.

1. In Revelation 1:16, what is the appearance of the Lord's
   face?

Strange as it may seem, at this juncture Moses and Elijah appear
on the scene discussing something with Christ (Matthew 17:3). How
can this be? A mystery surrounds the final nature of Moses' body (Jude
1:9; Deuteronomy 34:5–6); Elijah was translated without experiencing
death (2 Kings 2:11). This is why they can appear here. This is a glorious kingdom scene—the two ancient visitors appear in glory. But it
is also a preparation for death.

2. Read Luke 9:31. What were Moses, Elijah, and Christ
   discussing?

These two men are intensely interested in Christ's upcoming sufferings. But this is not so with Peter. In his enthusiasm, he wants to
make this site a shrine for the worship of all three (v. 4) and thus avoid
the cross. In his proposal, he foolishly places Moses and Elijah in the
same class with the Messiah. Peter, the rock on which the church was
to be built, has a lot to learn. His misguided words draw down a bright
cloud. Out of it, Peter hears a voice.

3. Compare the words of the voice in Matthew 3:17 with
   that in 17:5. What is the difference in what they say?

Peter and the church built upon him and his revelation of the
Christ must no longer listen to Moses or Elijah, representing Israel's
Law and prophets. This is reminiscent of words that will later be
written to the church formed by Peter and the eleven in Jerusalem:
"Long ago God spoke to our ancestors in many and various ways by
the prophets, but in these last days he has spoken to us by the Son"
(Hebrews 1:1 NRSV).

Day Eighteen

Matthew 18:23–35

23 Therefore is the kingdom of heaven likened unto a certain king, which would take account of his servants.

24 And when he had begun to reckon, one was brought unto him, which owed him ten thousand talents.

25 But forasmuch as he had not to pay, his lord commanded him to be sold, and his wife, and children, and all that he had, and payment to be made.

26 The servant therefore fell down, and worshipped him, saying, Lord, have patience with me, and I will pay thee all.

27 Then the lord of that servant was moved with compassion, and loosed him, and forgave him the debt.

28 But the same servant went out, and found one of his fellowservants, which owed him an hundred pence: and he laid hands on him, and took him by the throat, saying, Pay me that thou owest.

29 And his fellowservant fell down at his feet, and besought him, saying, Have patience with me, and I will pay thee all.

30 And he would not: but went and cast him into prison, till he should pay the debt.

31 So when his fellowservants saw what was done, they were very sorry, and came and told unto their lord all that was done.

32 Then his lord, after that he had called him, said unto him, O thou wicked servant, I forgave thee all that debt, because thou desiredst me:

33 Shouldest not thou also have had compassion on thy fellowservant, even as I had pity on thee?

34 And his lord was wroth, and delivered him to the tormentors, till he should pay all that was due unto him.

35 So likewise shall my heavenly Father do also unto you, if ye from your hearts forgive not every one his brother their trespasses.

The Withdrawal of Israel's Pardon

This parable of the ten thousand–talent debtor illustrates the true meaning of pardon, which in the New Testament is sometimes translated *forgiveness*. This man's great debt was canceled, but the pardon was later recalled. The permanence of his pardon depended upon his conduct. This is typical of the gospel of the kingdom of the heavens.

Gentiles who have believed the gospel of God's grace in Christ are justified. Our judicial standing before God is that there is no charge against us. God, as judge, has cleared us of guilt by the blood of Christ (Romans 3:24). But a judge cannot pardon. This is the sole privilege of a governor or king. Matthew concerns the kingdom of the heavens, so its king proclaims the pardon of Israel's sins. A pardon is probational. It may be withdrawn because of improper conduct. This parable is about the withdrawal of Israel's pardon.

1. Read Matthew 6:12. What is the standard that God uses to pardon sins in the kingdom?

2. In Ephesians 1:7, what causes the forgiveness of sins in the present day?

Thousands of Jews were pardoned in the days recorded in the early chapters of Acts (2:41; 4:4). These are represented by the ten thousand–talent debtor in this parable. They were the corrupt generation who had crucified Jesus Christ and so were under immense obligations to God (2:23, 40). Nevertheless, in compassion, God pardoned their sins (Acts 2:38).

The nations of this world had none of Israel's spiritual light and privilege. They didn't owe God nearly so much. The debtor who owes only one hundred pence represents them in this parable. The pardoned believers in Israel had no thought of sharing God's mercy with the despised Gentiles. Peter had to be powerfully persuaded by a vision from God before he would minister to the Gentile Cornelius (10:1–48).

3. Read Acts 11:1–3. What was the reaction of the believers in Jerusalem after Peter brought the gospel to Gentiles?

These same pardoned believers sought to murder Paul for the very mention of the name *Gentiles* (22:21–23). Consequently, their pardon was revoked. That is, Israel's kingdom was put on hold. Only after the full number of the Gentiles comes into God's salvation by grace will all Israel be saved (Romans 11:25–26).

However, do not think that Israel is forever lost. Recall God's words: "So I ask, have they stumbled so as to fall? By no means! But through their stumbling salvation has come to the Gentiles, so as to make Israel jealous. Now if their stumbling means riches for the world, and if their defeat means riches for Gentiles, how much more will their full inclusion mean!" (Romans 11:11–12 NRSV).

Day Nineteen

Matthew 20:17–28

17 And Jesus going up to Jerusalem took the twelve disciples apart in the way, and said unto them,

18 Behold, we go up to Jerusalem; and the Son of man shall be betrayed unto the chief priests and unto the scribes, and they shall condemn him to death,

19 And shall deliver him to the Gentiles to mock, and to scourge, and to crucify him: and the third day he shall rise again.

20 Then came to him the mother of Zebedees children with her sons, worshipping him, and desiring a certain thing of him.

21 And he said unto her, What wilt thou? She saith unto him, Grant that these my two sons may sit, the one on thy right hand, and the other on the left, in thy kingdom.

22 But Jesus answered and said, Ye know not what ye ask. Are ye able to drink of the cup that I shall drink of, and to be baptized with the baptism that I am baptized with? They say unto him, We are able.

23 And he saith unto them, Ye shall drink indeed of my cup, and be baptized with the baptism that I am baptized with: but to sit on my right hand, and on my left, is not mine to give, but it shall be given to them for whom it is prepared of my Father.

24 And when the ten heard it, they were moved with indignation against the two brethren.

25 But Jesus called them unto him, and said, Ye know that the princes of the Gentiles exercise dominion over them, and they that are great exercise authority upon them.

26 But it shall not be so among you: but whosoever will be great among you, let him be your minister;

27 And whosoever will be chief among you, let him be your servant:

28 Even as the Son of man came not to be ministered unto, but to minister, and to give his life a ransom for many.

Blinded by Ambition

Sad irony colors this passage of scripture. Jesus gives the disciples their clearest view of the humiliation and death that awaits him in Jerusalem. Yet, they persist in the thought that the kingdom of the heavens is near and are striving with each other for positions of authority in it.

1. In Matthew 20:18–19, what are the seven steps of the Lord's suffering?

James and John were the sons of Zebedee (Mark 10:35). Jesus called them the sons of thunder to indicate their stormy disposition (3:17). They seem to be the most ambitious and selfish of all the apostles. Their mother is rather pushy as well, requesting the best positions in the kingdom for her sons.

2. Jesus is going to be humiliated. James and John want to be exalted. What is Paul seeking in Philippians 3:10 that these two disciples cannot yet see?

Only those who drink Christ's cup can share Christ's honors. So, he grants them a sip of his sorrow (Matthew 20:23). James was the first of the two to follow the Lord when Herod put him to death by the sword (Acts 12:1). John lived longer, though the gentleness and love of his writings indicate that the fires of suffering refined his passionate character.

The restoration of two blind men to sight shows there is hope for John, James, and all the disciples (20:29–34). They were blinded by ambition and could not see the one vital vista of history, the cross of Christ. Although they followed him to Jerusalem in the flesh, they could not follow him in spirit.

3. Read Luke 24:36–48. When did Jesus open the minds of the disciples to understand the scriptures?

Day Twenty

Matthew 21:6–17

6 And the disciples went, and did as Jesus commanded them,

7 And brought the ass, and the colt, and put on them their clothes, and they set him thereon.

8 And a very great multitude spread their garments in the way; others cut down branches from the trees, and strawed them in the way.

9 And the multitudes that went before, and that followed, cried, saying, Hosanna to the son of David: Blessed is he that cometh in the name of the Lord; Hosanna in the highest.

10 And when he was come into Jerusalem, all the city was moved, saying, Who is this?

11 And the multitude said, This is Jesus the prophet of Nazareth of Galilee.

12 And Jesus went into the temple of God, and cast out all them that sold and bought in the temple, and overthrew the tables of the moneychangers, and the seats of them that sold doves,

13 And said unto them, It is written, My house shall be called the house of prayer; but ye have made it a den of thieves.

14 And the blind and the lame came to him in the temple; and he healed them.

15 And when the chief priests and scribes saw the wonderful things that he did, and the children crying in the temple, and saying, Hosanna to the son of David; they were sore displeased,

16 And said unto him, Hearest thou what these say? And Jesus saith unto them, Yea; have ye never read, Out of the mouth of babes and sucklings thou hast perfected praise?

17 And he left them, and went out of the city into Bethany; and he lodged there.

The Cleansing of the Temple

Jesus' approach to Jerusalem is triumphant even though the Son of David is riding on the colt of an ass. But the celebration is limited to the humble folk outside the city walls. Inside, the citizens of the City of David don't recognize their king. Instead, they ask "Who is this?" The best answer they can get is "This is the prophet." So begins the last week of the Lord's life.

Jesus' first act is to cleanse the temple of idolatry. He drives out the buyers, sellers, moneychangers, and sacrifice vendors (Matthew 21:12). In those days, the temple tax had to be paid by even the poorest of the people (17:24). Collectors were in each city and in the Temple. Here were currency exchanges to convert foreign coin to that acceptable in the Temple. This was done at a profit.

1. Colossians 3:5 defines covetousness (greed). What is this definition?

All this occurs in the court of the nations, which is outside the sanctuary proper. This is where converts to Judaism from other nations pray, worship, and bring gifts and sacrifices. It is not intended for merchandising or banking. It is a place for God to give to humanity not for man to rob his fellow man.

Jesus cleansed the sanctuary twice. These illustrate the two aspects of Jesus' divine commission—priest and king. The first Temple cleansing is found only in John 2:13–22. There, acting as a priest, he declared, "Destroy this temple, and in three days I will raise it up," referring to his own sacrificial death and resurrection (v. 19, 21–22).

2. Read Exodus 12:15. What were the Israelites required to remove from their houses before the Passover celebration?

John shows Jesus in his priestly function cleansing the Temple from the leaven of covetousness. At that time, the poorest house in the land was being cleansed of leaven, but Israel's priests allowed spiritual leaven to flourish in the courts of the Lord. They supposedly abhorred idolatry yet here it is in the house of God! Jesus did what the priests should have done and cleansed his Father's house in preparation for the Passover.

The second cleansing shows him as Israel's king (Matthew 21:12–13). The silent submission of the merchant-robbers is evidence of Christ's kingly majesty and might. If he had done this out of violent passion, he would have been met by physical force and defeated. But the covetous idolaters of Israel are awed by the righteous wrath of the glorious king, and they flee from his presence.

3. Read Isaiah 56:7. How does Isaiah describe the Temple?

4. By Jeremiah's day, what had the Temple become? (Read Jeremiah 7:11.)

Day Twenty-One

Matthew 22:15–22

15 Then went the Pharisees, and took counsel how they might entangle him in his talk.

16 And they sent out unto him their disciples with the Herodians, saying, Master, we know that thou art true, and teachest the way of God in truth, neither carest thou for any man: for thou regardest not the person of men.

17 Tell us therefore, What thinkest thou? Is it lawful to give tribute unto Caesar, or not?

18 But Jesus perceived their wickedness, and said, Why tempt ye me, ye hypocrites?

19 Shew me the tribute money. And they brought unto him a penny.

20 And he saith unto them, Whose is this image and superscription?

21 They say unto him, Caesar's. Then saith he unto them, Render therefore unto Caesar the things which are Caesar's; and unto God the things that are God's.

22 When they had heard these words, they marvelled, and left him, and went their way.

The Question of Taxes

Matthew 22 records various attempts by Israel's leaders to entrap Jesus in political crimes or theological heresy. Here the Pharisees and Herodians pose a question about taxes. The Pharisees, a sect of fundamentalist religionists, had commanded the respect of Israelites for 150 years because of their zeal and rigid observance of the Law of Moses. The Herodians were Jewish supporters of Herod, the Roman tetrarch. Ordinarily these two groups, religious and political, would have been at odds, but here they unite around a common threat, Jesus of Nazareth. Jesus answers their question and convicts them of one of the crimes that they hope to pin on him. That is, *they* pay taxes to Rome.

His mere presence among them as the Messiah of Israel has shown how little authority they have. So, they must somehow lure him into conflict with the people or the government. Then they might destroy him. To this end, they formulate a leading question: "Is it lawful to pay taxes to Caesar or not?" (v. 17). If he answers, "Yes," the Pharisees will spread this among the people, who hate the Roman taxes, and his popularity will wane. If he says, "No," the Herodians will report him to the government and he will be tried for treason. Instead, he catches them in their own question.

1. Read Matthew 17:24–27. Did Jesus pay taxes?

Therefore, Jesus asks, "Show me the coin used for the tax." That which bears the image of Caesar belongs to Caesar. That which bears the image of God belongs to God (vv. 20–21; Genesis 1:26). Sure enough, they produce a Roman denarius. Their use of this Roman currency reveals their subjection to Rome—they must give their emperor's coin to their emperor.

2. In Matthew 22:19–20, what bears the image of Caesar?

3. In Genesis 1:26, what bears the image of God?

Day Twenty-Two

Matthew 23:13–29

13 But woe unto you, scribes and Pharisees, hypocrites! for ye shut up the kingdom of heaven against men: for ye neither go in yourselves, neither suffer ye them that are entering to go in.

14 Woe unto you, scribes and Pharisees, hypocrites! for ye devour widows' houses, and for a pretence make long prayer: therefore ye shall receive the greater damnation.

15 Woe unto you, scribes and Pharisees, hypocrites! for ye compass sea and land to make one proselyte, and when he is made, ye make him twofold more the child of hell than yourselves.

16 Woe unto you, ye blind guides, which say, Whosoever shall swear by the temple, it is nothing; but whosoever shall swear by the gold of the temple, he is a debtor!

17 Ye fools and blind: for whether is greater, the gold, or the temple that sanctifieth the gold? . . .

23 Woe unto you, scribes and Pharisees, hypocrites! for ye pay tithe of mint and anise and cummin, and have omitted the weightier matters of the law, judgment, mercy, and faith: these ought ye to have done, and not to leave the other undone.

24 Ye blind guides, which strain at a gnat, and swallow a camel.

25 Woe unto you, scribes and Pharisees, hypocrites! for ye make clean the outside of the cup and of the platter, but within they are full of extortion and excess.

26 Thou blind Pharisee, cleanse first that which is within the cup and platter, that the outside of them may be clean also.

27 Woe unto you, scribes and Pharisees, hypocrites! for ye are like unto whited sepulchres, which indeed appear beautiful outward, but are within full of dead men's bones, and of all uncleanness.

28 Even so ye also outwardly appear righteous unto men, but within ye are full of hypocrisy and iniquity.

29 Woe unto you, scribes and Pharisees, hypocrites! because ye build the tombs of the prophets, and garnish the sepulchres of the righteous,

The Seven Woes

Jesus Christ began his kingdom ministry with a nine-fold benediction. These are commonly called the beatitudes. They address various sorts of people:

1. The poor in spirit (Matthew 5:3)

2. The mourners (v. 4)

3. The meek (v. 5)

4. Those who are hungering and thirsting for righteousness (v. 6)

5. The merciful (v. 7)

6. The pure in heart (v. 8)

7. The peacemakers (v. 9)

8. Those who are persecuted because of righteousness (v. 10)

9. Those reproached falsely on his account (v. 11)

The Lord closes his kingdom ministry by articulating seven woes on the Pharisees who:

1. Hinder others from entering the kingdom (23:13)

2. Recruit for their own party (v. 15)

3. Elevate that which is hallowed above that which hallows (v. 16–22)

4. Distort the extent of God's rules (v. 23–24)

5. Cleanse the outside but leave the inside full of filth (v. 25–26)

6. Appear righteous, but are lawless within (v. 27–28)

7. Pretend to be more righteous than their forefathers yet actually go beyond them in iniquity (v. 29–31)

The kingdom of the heavens is locked to Israel at the time these words are spoken. It will not be reopened until the day of Pentecost when Peter uses the keys entrusted to him (16:19). Later, the Pharisees and scribes again lock their nation out of the kingdom by refusing the testimony of the apostles (Acts 28:25–29). Therefore, the earthly kingdom is now locked. It will not again be opened until Christ comes in glory.

1. Read Acts 2:38. What are the two keys Peter used to unlock the kingdom for Israel?

2. Who else, early in the gospel accounts, used these same devices to give Israel entrance into the kingdom? (Read Mark 1:4.)

3. Read the following verses and find the portion from Isaiah that is used as the lock on the kingdom: Matthew 13:13–15; Mark 4:10–12; Luke 8:10–11; John 12:36–43; Acts 28:25–29; Romans 11:8.

Day Twenty-Three

Matthew 24:3–14

3 And as he sat upon the mount of Olives, the disciples came unto him privately, saying, Tell us, when shall these things be? and what shall be the sign of thy coming, and of the end of the world?

4 And Jesus answered and said unto them, Take heed that no man deceive you.

5 For many shall come in my name, saying, I am Christ; and shall deceive many.

6 And ye shall hear of wars and rumours of wars: see that ye be not troubled: for all these things must come to pass, but the end is not yet.

7 For nation shall rise against nation, and kingdom against kingdom: and there shall be famines, and pestilences, and earthquakes, in divers places.

8 All these are the beginning of sorrows.

9 Then shall they deliver you up to be afflicted, and shall kill you: and ye shall be hated of all nations for my name's sake.

10 And then shall many be offended, and shall betray one another, and shall hate one another.

11 And many false prophets shall rise, and shall deceive many.

12 And because iniquity shall abound, the love of many shall wax cold.

13 But he that shall endure unto the end, the same shall be saved.

14 And this gospel of the kingdom shall be preached in all the world for a witness unto all nations; and then shall the end come.

The First Four Seals of Revelation

Matthew 24 presents a prophetic outline of events that are to occur before the kingdom can come. Jesus does not mention the present blessings of God's grace, because he is ministering to Israel. So, he overlooks all that occurs during the era of Israel's unbelief (see Romans 11). It is as if the end of this age follows immediately after the close of Acts. The time that has passed since then is a pause in God's plan for Israel.

1. Read Romans 11:25. When will Israel again believe?

The Bible is more harmonious than most people realize. For example: Jesus Christ's prophecy in Matthew 24 describes the so-called four horses of the apocalypse. They are the first four of the seven seals depicted in Revelation 6:

- "I watched as the Lamb opened the first of the seven seals. . .I looked, and there before me was a white horse! Its rider held a bow, and he was given a crown, and he rode out as a conqueror bent on conquest" (Revelation 6:2 NIV).

  Christ says there will be many false Messiahs (Matthew 24:5). Some of these have already come (1 John 2:18). But this one is the ultimate—an imitation of the true one. This white horse and rider conquers the nations to unite them against God, all the while leading them to believe that he is the man of destiny who is able to solve humanity's problems. The true white horseman is the Messiah who appears in Revelation 19:11–16.

- "When the Lamb opened the second seal, I heard the second living creature say, 'Come!' Then another horse came out, a fiery red one. Its rider was given power to take peace from the earth and to make men slay each other. To him was given a large sword" (vv. 3–4 NIV).

  This red horse and rider take peace from the earth. It corresponds with the wars and rumors of wars mentioned in Matthew 24:6–7. These wars do not seem to resemble our modern conflicts where nations send small contingents of soldiers against each other. Verse seven says whole nations and kingdoms will rise against each other indicating a world war with universal conscription.

- "When the Lamb opened the third seal. . .and there before me was a black horse! Its rider was holding a pair of scales in his hand. Then I heard what sounded like a voice among the four living creatures, saying, 'A quart of wheat for a day's wages, and three quarts of barley for a day's wages, and do not damage the oil and the wine!' " (Revelation 6:5–6 NIV).

Jesus said, "there shall be famines" (Matthew 24:7). These famines are the third seal when wheat and barley will be worth many times their normal value.

- "When the Lamb opened the fourth seal. . .I looked, and there before me was a pale horse! Its rider was named Death, and Hades was following close behind him. They were given power over a fourth of the earth to kill by sword, famine and plague, and by the wild beasts of the earth" (Revelation 6:7–8 NIV).

  Here, the pale horse of the fourth seal brings the pestilences mentioned by Jesus in Matthew 24:7. (See also Luke 21:11.)

2. As of the day of this writing, the US Census bureau estimates the world's population to be 6,399,895,628. How many people will die when the first four seals are opened (see Revelation 6:8)?

3. Compare Matthew 24:9 with Revelation 6:9. Both these verses describe the same feature of the great tribulation (Matthew 24:21). What is that feature?

Day Twenty-Four

Matthew 25:31–40

31 When the Son of man shall come in his glory, and all the holy angels with him, then shall he sit upon the throne of his glory:

32 And before him shall be gathered all nations: and he shall separate them one from another, as a shepherd divideth his sheep from the goats:

33 And he shall set the sheep on his right hand, but the goats on the left.

34 Then shall the King say unto them on his right hand, Come, ye blessed of my Father, inherit the kingdom prepared for you from the foundation of the world:

35 For I was an hungred, and ye gave me meat: I was thirsty, and ye gave me drink: I was a stranger, and ye took me in:

36 Naked, and ye clothed me: I was sick, and ye visited me: I was in prison, and ye came unto me.

37 Then shall the righteous answer him, saying, Lord, when saw we thee an hungred, and fed thee? or thirsty, and gave thee drink?

38 When saw we thee a stranger, and took thee in? or naked, and clothed thee?

39 Or when saw we thee sick, or in prison, and came unto thee?

40 And the King shall answer and say unto them, Verily I say unto you, Inasmuch as ye have done it unto one of the least of these my brethren, ye have done it unto me.

The Judging of the Nations

There is not simply one judgment mentioned in the scriptures. There are several. They differ as to time, place, character, participants, and purpose.

1. Compare Romans 6:6 with 2 Corinthians 5:15. Who was judged in the cross of Christ?

2. Read Revelation 20:12. What is the basis for the judgment of the unbelievers at the great white throne?

The judgment presented in Matthew 25:31–46 occurs between the times of the cross and the white throne. The details are as follows:

- Time? This judgment occurs at the beginning of the kingdom when Christ comes in glory. The great white throne session does not take place until after the thousand years.

- Place? This judgment is on the earth. However, the earth will flee before the great white throne (Revelation 20:11).

- Character? The nations here are judged, not for their sins as in the future, but according to their treatment of Israel during the time of their affliction (Matthew 25:39–40).

- Participants? Living nations will appear before the Son of Man (Matthew 25:31–32). Only the dead come before the one who will sit on the great white throne (Revelation 20:12).

- Purpose? When God judges the earth during the time of great tribulation (Matthew 24:21) the greatest act of righteousness will be to feed and shelter the oppressed people of Israel—the Lord's brethren (25:40). This judgment rewards the nations who aided Israel and punishes those who did not.

By this time, Christ will have returned and gathered his beloved Israel to himself. Israel will have looked on the one whom they pierced (Zechariah 12:10; John 19:37). The nation will have been born in a day (Isaiah 66:8). Therefore, each faithful Israelite stands in the place of Christ toward the nations. But those who help them in their suffering do so in the face of mortal danger. They may be called to account by the powers that oppose Israel and her Messiah.

This tribunal is not concerned with the ultimate destiny of those who are on trial, but with their place in the kingdom's thousand years. Most of the citizens of the kingdom will be Gentiles who are subject to Israel politically and religiously. Nevertheless, they will be the recipients of much blessing. All that they receive comes to them through the blessed nation.

3. In Romans 11:11–12, why do we enjoy salvation in this age?

We, who are Christ's, have every reason to treat the Jews with grace today, but our conduct toward them is not a factor in our destiny. We do not enter the earthly kingdom. We have a higher and more honorable inheritance in the heavenly places (Ephesians 1:3; 2:2–7).

Day Twenty-Five

Matthew 26:30–41

30 And when they had sung an hymn, they went out into the mount of Olives.

31 Then saith Jesus unto them, All ye shall be offended because of me this night: for it is written, I will smite the shepherd, and the sheep of the flock shall be scattered abroad.

32 But after I am risen again, I will go before you into Galilee.

33 Peter answered and said unto him, Though all men shall be offended because of thee, yet will I never be offended.

34 Jesus said unto him, Verily I say unto thee, That this night, before the cock crow, thou shalt deny me thrice.

35 Peter said unto him, Though I should die with thee, yet will I not deny thee. Likewise also said all the disciples.

36 Then cometh Jesus with them unto a place called Gethsemane, and saith unto the disciples, Sit ye here, while I go and pray yonder.

37 And he took with him Peter and the two sons of Zebedee, and began to be sorrowful and very heavy.

38 Then saith he unto them, My soul is exceeding sorrowful, even unto death: tarry ye here, and watch with me.

39 And he went a little farther, and fell on his face, and prayed, saying, O my Father, if it be possible, let this cup pass from me: nevertheless not as I will, but as thou wilt.

40 And he cometh unto the disciples, and findeth them asleep, and saith unto Peter, What, could ye not watch with me one hour?

41 Watch and pray, that ye enter not into temptation: the spirit indeed is willing, but the flesh is weak.

The Will of God in the Garden

The Lord is clear that all of the disciples will be offended, snared, and renounce him on the night of his arrest and trial (Matthew 26:31). Immediately, Peter denies the Lord's word and begins his fall. He refuses to believe that when the Lord said, "All," he meant *all*. Peter can't imagine how this can include him. In this way, he exalts himself above the rest of the disciples and so invites the fate of all who walk in pride.

1. In Proverbs 16:18, what can cause a person's fall and destruction?

Peter's overconfidence is still among us today in bold declarations of loyalty and devotion to God. If all these were carried out, the whole world would be transformed in one generation. However, there is no doubt that these affirmations are honest. Peter fully intends to stand by his Lord to the death. But he does not know himself or the weakness of the human will. Peter is an example to us so that we will not follow him in his pride and fall. This is the third time Peter is so brash. A fourth time is yet to come:

• Peter was first foolishly bold when Jesus came to the disciple's boat in a storm on the Sea of Galilee: "Peter got down out of the boat, walked on the water and came toward Jesus" (Matthew 14:30 NIV).

• The next time was when the Lord was transfigured: "Peter said to Jesus, 'Lord, it is good for us to be here. If you wish, I will put up three shelters—one for you, one for Moses and one for Elijah' " (17:4).

• Finally, when Jesus appeared in resurrection on the seashore: "As soon as Simon Peter heard him say, "It is the Lord," he wrapped his outer garment around him (for he had taken it off) and jumped into the water" (John 21:7).

2. In Matthew 14:30, what was Jesus' immediate reaction to Peter's brashness?

3. What did Jesus do after Peter's stupid proposal in Matthew 17:4? (Read 17:7.)

Jesus is not so bold as Peter. Here in the Garden of Gethsemane, he is about to face horrendous battle with the forces of darkness and their human subjects. He is the Son of God and has never yet suffered a defeat in his human life. Yet, does he boast like Peter? No, instead he prays to be spared: "My Father, if it is possible, let this cup pass from me" (Matthew 26:39). It was not his will to go to the cross. Until now, Christ's will and the Father's had been in perfect harmony (John 10:30). He delights in God's will even though it brings him opposition and hate. Yet, the terrors of the curse and the abandonment of God that await him on the cross are beyond the agreement of his will, despite his matchless loyalty and devotion. But Christ did not come to do his own will. So he prays, "My Father, if this cannot pass unless I drink it, your will be done" (Matthew 26:42 NRSV).

4. Read Hebrews 10:5–10. Why did Jesus Christ come to live among the human race?

Day Twenty-Six

Matthew 27:27–44

27 Then the soldiers of the governor took Jesus into the common hall, and gathered unto him the whole band of soldiers.

28 And they stripped him, and put on him a scarlet robe.

29 And when they had platted a crown of thorns, they put it upon his head, and a reed in his right hand: and they bowed the knee before him, and mocked him, saying, Hail, King of the Jews! . . .

33 And when they were come unto a place called Golgotha, that is to say, a place of a skull,

34 They gave him vinegar to drink mingled with gall: and when he had tasted thereof, he would not drink.

35 And they crucified him, and parted his garments, casting lots: that it might be fulfilled which was spoken by the prophet, They parted my garments among them, and upon my vesture did they cast lots.

36 And sitting down they watched him there;

37 And set up over his head his accusation written, THIS IS JESUS THE KING OF THE JEWS.

38 Then were there two thieves crucified with him, one on the right hand, and another on the left.

39 And they that passed by reviled him, wagging their heads,

40 And saying, Thou that destroyest the temple, and buildest it in three days, save thyself. If thou be the Son of God, come down from the cross.

41 Likewise also the chief priests mocking him, with the scribes and elders, said,

42 He saved others; himself he cannot save. If he be the King of Israel, let him now come down from the cross, and we will believe him.

43 He trusted in God; let him deliver him now, if he will have him: for he said, I am the Son of God.

44 The thieves also, which were crucified with him, cast the same in his teeth.

The Prophecy of the Crucifiers

The whole scene around the cross is vibrant with the presence of God. Certainly, this is seen in Christ, the victim. It is also seen in the few who followed him there (Matthew 27:55–56). However, the words of those who hated him also convey godliness.

1. Read Matthew 27:15–19. Who is the only person among the actors in the tragedy of Jesus' death that pleads the cause of the Christ?

2. In Matthew 27:21, what is the name of the first man who was delivered from death by the crucifixion of Christ?

3. 1 Timothy 1:15 tells of the chief of all sinners who was saved by Christ. Who is this?

The crucifiers of Jesus Christ spoke great truths that they could not have understood:

• The soldiers of the governor dress him in a scarlet robe, signifying his attainment to the imperial Roman throne. They crown him with thorns and thrust a reed into his hand for a royal scepter. Then they kneel, saying, "Hail! King of the Jews!" (vv. 27–31 NRSV). The crowd that shouted, "Crucify him!" (v. 22) should have worshiped their Messiah with such words.

• People observing the spectacle of the Lord's execution gamble for his clothes (v. 35). This fulfills the scriptures: "They part my garments among them, and cast lots upon my vesture" (Psalm 22:18).

• Passers-by shake their heads and deride him. "You who would destroy the temple and build it in three days. . ." (Matthew 27:40). But they are the ones who are demolishing the true temple of God (26:61).

• The chief priests are present here at the sacrifice of the Lamb of God (John 1:29). They cannot help but express this precious truth: "He saved others; he cannot save himself" (v. 42). Yet, they are the ones who need salvation. This salvation will never come if he saves himself by coming down from that cross.

- The chief priests of Israel give a brief sermon at the foot of the cross of shame (vv. 41–43). "He is the King of Israel," they mock, "let him come down from the cross now, and we will believe in him" (v. 42). If they cannot believe the resurrection of Lazarus (John 11:43–44), they will believe nothing (Luke 16:30–31).

- "He trusts in God," they preach. "Let God deliver him now if he wants to; for he said, 'I am God's Son' " (v. 43). Yet, they'd certainly heard of Jesus' remark to their colleague Nicodemus: "God so loved the world that he gave his only Son, so that everyone who believes in him may not perish but may have eternal life" (John 3:16 NRSV). He was on that cross to deliver them and so would not violate God's will and deliver himself.

4. At the beginning and the end of Jesus' journey to the cross, the same proclamation was made. Compare Matthew 17:5 and 27:54. What is that proclamation?

Day Twenty-Seven

Matthew 27:45–54

45 Now from the sixth hour there was darkness over all the land unto the ninth hour.

46 And about the ninth hour Jesus cried with a loud voice, saying, Eli, Eli, lama sabachthani? that is to say, My God, my God, why hast thou forsaken me?

47 Some of them that stood there, when they heard that, said, This man calleth for Elias.

48 And straightway one of them ran, and took a spunge, and filled it with vinegar, and put it on a reed, and gave him to drink.

49 The rest said, Let be, let us see whether Elias will come to save him.

50 Jesus, when he had cried again with a loud voice, yielded up the ghost.

51 And, behold, the veil of the temple was rent in twain from the top to the bottom; and the earth did quake, and the rocks rent;

52 And the graves were opened; and many bodies of the saints which slept arose,

53 And came out of the graves after his resurrection, and went into the holy city, and appeared unto many.

54 Now when the centurion, and they that were with him, watching Jesus, saw the earthquake, and those things that were done, they feared greatly, saying, Truly this was the Son of God.

Darkness at the Crucifixion

A dread darkness falls on the earth at noon of the crucifixion day. This indicates the removal of the divine presence from the wonderful sufferer there. This withdrawal is so much more awful than the opposition of his enemies or the desertion of his friends. Until darkness enveloped him, Jesus had always lived in the light of God's smile.

1. Read Galatians 3:13. What did Jesus Christ become when he hung on the cross?

It is as if the fire from above entered into Jesus' bones as he hung on the cross (Lamentations 1:13). This is when the Lord bruises him (Isaiah 53:10). These dark hours settle the question of sin.

2. According to 2 Corinthians 5:21, what was Christ made on the cross? What did you become as a result?

Man, at the command of Satan, crucifies him. God abandons him. In these hours, Jesus is the most forlorn and forsaken creature in the universe. When you see God arrayed against Christ, you can appreciate how much he is for you now. Only when light returns to the landscape can he cry out to God.

3. According to Matthew 27:46, what did Jesus cry out to the Father at three o'clock on the afternoon of the crucifixion?

The question Jesus asks of his God is unanswerable unless he is suffering for the sins of others. Otherwise, God would never abandon him. It was for our sake that he endured the cross despising the shame (Hebrews 12:2). He not only endured the physical pain, the mental torture, and the moral degradation caused by his fellow man. He also had to absorb the indescribably deep despair of the enmity of his God.

DAY TWENTY-EIGHT

Matthew 28:1–20

1 In the end of the sabbath, as it began to dawn toward the first day of the week, came Mary Magdalene and the other Mary to see the sepulchre.

2 And, behold, there was a great earthquake: for the angel of the Lord descended from heaven, and came and rolled back the stone from the door, and sat upon it.

3 His countenance was like lightning, and his raiment white as snow:

4 And for fear of him the keepers did shake, and became as dead men.

5 And the angel answered and said unto the women, Fear not ye: for I know that ye seek Jesus, which was crucified.

6 He is not here: for he is risen, as he said. Come, see the place where the Lord lay. . . .

9 And as they went to tell his disciples, behold, Jesus met them, saying, All hail. And they came and held him by the feet, and worshipped him.

10 Then said Jesus unto them, Be not afraid: go tell my brethren that they go into Galilee, and there shall they see me. . . .

16 Then the eleven disciples went away into Galilee, into a mountain where Jesus had appointed them.

17 And when they saw him, they worshipped him: but some doubted.

18 And Jesus came and spake unto them, saying, All power is given unto me in heaven and in earth.

19 Go ye therefore, and teach all nations, baptizing them in the name of the Father, and of the Son, and of the Holy Ghost:

20 Teaching them to observe all things whatsoever I have commanded you: and, lo, I am with you always, even unto the end of the world. Amen.

Gentiles in Matthew

The book of Matthew shows that the Messiah was sent only to the lost sheep of the house of Israel (15:24). Therefore, Jesus would not let his apostles go to the nations or the Samaritans (10:5). Still, the few appearances of Gentiles in Matthew are significant.

Four gentile women are seen in Christ's genealogy (1:3, 5, 6):

- Tamar's sin introduced her into the line of the king's ancestry (Genesis 38).

- Rahab came in by faith (Joshua 2).

- Ruth's case shows grace, triumphing over the law that banned a Moabite from the congregation of the Lord (Ruth 1–4; Deuteronomy 23:3).

- Bathsheba is a reminder of David's great sin and shows grace reigning despite sin (2 Samuel 11:1–12:24).

The magi, who worship Christ, contrast with Herod, who seeks his life (2:1–12). A centurion shows a level of faith that is unknown in Israel (8:5–12). He believed without a miraculous sign or even the Lord's presence.

1. In Psalm 107:20 and in the case of the centurion's servant in Matthew 8:5–13, what does the Lord use to heal?

The persistent Canaanite woman is admired for her confidence in Christ (15:21–28). Pilate and his wife refuse responsibility when the Jews want an official condemnation of the Messiah (27:11, 24). The centurion at the cross acknowledges that he is the Son of God (27:54).

2. In Ephesians 2:12, what five items describe the condition of the Gentiles in Matthew?

3. Read John 19:12. Why did Pilate give the religious leaders permission to crucify Jesus?

At the end of Matthew's account of the Lord's life, after all authority on earth is in the hands of the king, the disciples are commissioned to go and make disciples of all nations (Matthew 28:19–20). However, this cannot occur until the kingdom comes to Israel (Revelation 11:15).

Answer Key to Questions in Matthew

Day Question

1. 1. Boaz and Ruth.
   2. David, Israel's king.
   3. Gold, frankincense, and myrrh.
   4. God's eternal power and divine nature.

2. 1. The wind.
   2. As breath.
   3. The sound of the rush of a violent wind and divided tongues of fire.

3. 1. It crushes them.
   2. The kingdom has no end.
   3. Righteousness, peace, and joy in the Holy Spirit.

4. 1. He cites the generosity of God in nature.
   2. Live in love.
   3. He cites the love and sacrifice of Christ.

5. 1. God's name (v. 9), the kingdom of the heavens, and God's will (v. 10).
   2. Food (v. 11), forgiveness from past failures (v. 12), escape from future trials (v. 13), and deliverance from the power of the evil one (v. 13).
   3. Matthew 6:12 is conditional; in Ephesians 1:7 forgiveness is free.

6. 1. The Psalmist struggled under a burden with the help of God.
   2. If you seek the kingdom of God, then all these things will be given to you.
   3. Peter got rid of the weight by casting it on the Lord.
   4. Paul replaces worry with peace and thanksgiving.

7. 1. Death.
   2. To test if you love the Lord your God with all your soul.
   3. In the foundation.

8. 1. The scribe knows no better than to call Jesus his teacher (KJV=master) rather than Messiah. This is the first time Jesus takes the title *Son of Man*.
   2. A living soul; a life-giving spirit.
   3. In Matthew, he wears a crown of thorns. In Revelation, he wears a crown of gold.
   4. The image of the man of dust; the image of the man of heaven.

9. 1. The dragon, which is Satan.
   2. Satan.
   3. Blasphemy against the Holy Spirit?the sin that cannot be pardoned in this age or that which is to come (Matthew 12:32).

10. 1. All the nations; Israel.
    2. After the Son of Man has been raised from the dead (see Acts 2:1).
    3. Repentance and baptism.
    4. The Gentiles.

11. 1. Because Herod had married Herodias, the wife of his brother Philip.
    2. John the Baptist.
    3. The coming of John the Baptist.

12. 1. They did not repent for the kingdom.
    2. Those who rejected Christ were not blinded by some act of their own. They do not see because God hides it from them.
    3. Let this mind be in you that was also in Christ Jesus.

13. 1. John the Baptist and Jesus.
    2. The Son of Man.
    3. Our heart.

14. 1. The world.
    2. No one seeks God. Not only so, Christ is not lost or hidden.
    3. The Son of Man came to seek out and save the lost.

15. 1. In verse 22, she calls him the Son of David. In verse 25, she calls him Lord.
    2. The circumcision—that is the people of Israel.
    3. She was an alien from the commonwealth of Israel and a stranger to the covenants of promise.
    4. The adoption, the glory, the covenants, the giving of the law, the worship, the promises, the patriarchs, and according to the flesh, the Messiah.

16. 1. The other eleven disciples are with Peter as the foundation of the New Jerusalem.
    2. Repentance and baptism.
    3. Peter is the apostle to the circumcision. Paul is the apostle to the Gentiles.

17. 1. The Lord's face is like the sun shining with full force.
    2. Jesus' upcoming departure (death) from Jerusalem.
    3. In 17:5, the words, "Listen to him" are added.

18. 1. One's sins are forgiven in relation to how one forgives others' sins.
    2. The riches of God's grace.
    3. They criticized Peter.

19. 1. Travel to Jerusalem, betrayal and condemnation by the Jews, mockery, scourging, and crucifixion by the Gentiles, resurrection.
    2. The sharing of Christ's sufferings and becoming like him in his death.
    3. After his resurrection.

20. 1. Covetousness is idolatry.
    2. All leaven.
    3. The house of God.
    4. A den of thieves.

21. 1. Yes. In this case, however, he paid the temple tax, not a tax to Rome.
    2. Money.
    3. Humanity.

22. 1. Repentance and baptism.
    2. John the Baptist.
    3. Isaiah 6:9–10.

23. 1. When the full number of the Gentiles has come in.
    2. 1,599,973,907 people; one quarter of the earth's population.
    3. The martyrdom of the faithful in Israel.

24. 1. The believers in Christ.
    2. Unbelievers are judged according to their works.
    3. Because Israel stumbled.

25. 1. Pride and a haughty spirit.
    2. He reached out his hand.
    3. He touched the disciples.
    4. To do God's will.

26 1. Pilate's wife.
    2. Barabbas—the name means "son of the father."
    3. Paul.
    4. This is the Son of God.

27. 1. Christ became a curse.
    2. He was made sin. We became God's righteousness.
    3. My God, my God, why have you forsaken me?

28. 1. The Lord's word heals.
    2. Without Christ, alien from the commonwealth of Israel, a stranger to the covenants of promise, having no hope, and without God in the world.
    3. The religious leaders threatened to report him to Caesar.

Introduction to
the Gospel of Mark

Mark reveals Jesus Christ as the model servant. It presents the intense activity of a diligent, hardworking man serving others. No sooner is a deed done than "straightway" he is engaged with another. This servant is introduced without a genealogy as found in Matthew and Luke. After all, he is nothing but a servant. His deeds are his qualifications. The reader is not so much engaged with Jesus Christ as with his work. We are told what he did, why, and how. Christ's birth, childhood, and youth are passed over because he was not engaged in service at those times. Mark's account begins straightway with Jesus' baptism into active ministry by John the Baptist.

Matthew emphasizes the king of Israel. Luke expands the view to show Christ blessing all mankind through Israel. The scope of Mark is broader still. It touches all creation. This account presents our Lord as a servant of Israel confirming God's promises. He comes to us through Israel and, after his resurrection, reaches out with blessing for the whole creation (Mark 16:15).

Mark's account has some significant omissions. Christ the servant is never addressed as Lord. Only after his resurrection is he given this title (16:19–20). Plus, the word *law* does not occur. The law does not measure his service, which exceeds all legal demands. Christ the servant does not expound the constitution of the kingdom as seen in Matthew chapters 5–7. It has fewer parables than the other gospels, and passages that display the majesty and glory of the Lord are omitted or abbreviated. He is, after all, a servant. Because of this, Christ avoids public notice in Mark (see 1:37–38; 7:24, 36; 8:25–26; 9:30). In this account, Christ's greatest glory is his humility.

Day Twenty-Nine

Mark 1:1–14

1 The beginning of the gospel of Jesus Christ, the Son of God;

2 As it is written in the prophets, Behold, I send my messenger before thy face, which shall prepare thy way before thee.

3 The voice of one crying in the wilderness, Prepare ye the way of the Lord, make his paths straight.

4 John did baptize in the wilderness, and preach the baptism of repentance for the remission of sins.

5 And there went out unto him all the land of Judaea, and they of Jerusalem, and were all baptized of him in the river of Jordan, confessing their sins.

6 And John was clothed with camel's hair, and with a girdle of a skin about his loins; and he did eat locusts and wild honey;

7 And preached, saying, There cometh one mightier than I after me, the latchet of whose shoes I am not worthy to stoop down and unloose.

8 I indeed have baptized you with water: but he shall baptize you with the Holy Ghost.

9 And it came to pass in those days, that Jesus came from Nazareth of Galilee, and was baptized of John in Jordan.

10 And straightway coming up out of the water, he saw the heavens opened, and the Spirit like a dove descending upon him:

11 And there came a voice from heaven, saying, Thou art my beloved Son, in whom I am well pleased.

12 And immediately the spirit driveth him into the wilderness.

13 And he was there in the wilderness forty days, tempted of Satan; and was with the wild beasts; and the angels ministered unto him.

14 Now after that John was put in prison, Jesus came into Galilee, preaching the gospel of the kingdom of God.

Jesus Christ and John the Baptist

As the son of a priest, John the Baptist could have inherited his father's priestly office and enjoyed all its privileges—a life of ease and comfort.

Yet, under the urge of the Holy Spirit, which filled him even before he was born, he gave up all this for the lowly and austere life of a Nazarite (Numbers 6:2–7).

1. Read Luke 1:41. What caused John to be filled with the Holy Spirit?

• As a Nazarite, John was not permitted to eat anything that came from the grapevine, the symbol of that which cheers the heart of God and man (Judges 9:13).

• Like Samson (Judges 13:5), he let his hair grow long, a symbol of weakness and dishonor (1 Corinthians 11:14).

• Instead of a priestly linen garment, he wore coarse camel's hair.

• Instead of living off the altar, eating the best of the sacrifices, and the tithes of the people, John survived on locusts and wild honey.

John the Baptist was much different that Jesus Christ: Christ was not a Nazarite. He drank wine, dressed as others did, and never wore long hair. While John lived in the wilderness, Jesus dwelt with his parents until the time for his ministry arrived.

But the contrast goes deeper than this. John came in the spirit and power of Elijah, an austere preacher of righteousness (Luke 1:17). Elijah had called fire down on men who were sent against him (2 Kings 1:10–12). The Lord's disciples wanted to do the same and consume the Samaritans for offending them (Luke 9:54). But Christ rebuked them. He did not come in the spirit of Elijah.

2. John 1:14 shows the spirit in which Jesus Christ came. In contrast to John the Baptist, what did Christ come with?

3. The disciples wanted to imitate Elijah and punish offenders. How did Jesus treat sinners? (Read John 3:17.)

DAY THIRTY

Mark 2:1–12

1 And again he entered into Capernaum after some days; and it was noised that he was in the house.

2 And straightway many were gathered together, insomuch that there was no room to receive them, no, not so much as about the door: and he preached the word unto them.

3 And they come unto him, bringing one sick of the palsy, which was borne of four.

4 And when they could not come nigh unto him for the press, they uncovered the roof where he was: and when they had broken it up, they let down the bed wherein the sick of the palsy lay.

5 When Jesus saw their faith, he said unto the sick of the palsy, Son, thy sins be forgiven thee.

6 But there was certain of the scribes sitting there, and reasoning in their hearts,

7 Why doth this man thus speak blasphemies? who can forgive sins but God only?

8 And immediately when Jesus perceived in his spirit that they so reasoned within themselves, he said unto them, Why reason ye these things in your hearts?

9 Whether is it easier to say to the sick of the palsy, Thy sins be forgiven thee; or to say, Arise, and take up thy bed, and walk?

10 But that ye may know that the Son of man hath power on earth to forgive sins, (he saith to the sick of the palsy,)

11 I say unto thee, Arise, and take up thy bed, and go thy way into thine house.

12 And immediately he arose, took up the bed, and went forth before them all; insomuch that they were all amazed, and glorified God, saying, We never saw it on this fashion.

Christ Forgives Sin

The healing of the paralyzed man in Mark 2:1–12 is the first time the Lord displays his authority to pardon sins. Sin paralyzes a person spiritually. So, the sign of his power to pardon it is to remove physical paralysis.

The scribes can easily see this with their physical eyes. If possible, this will open their spiritual eyes to the Lord's commission to pardon sins.

1. In Mark 2:12, what was the scribes' response to the healing of the paralytic?

2. Read Isaiah 43:25. What is the Lord's promise regarding Israel's sin?

Before this, Jesus had chosen four disciples: Peter and Andrew, James and John, were ordinary, hardworking fishermen (Mark 1:16–20). Human wisdom would suppose the Messiah would choose men of the highest character and reputation to be his apostles. However, after he announces his authority to pardon sins, the Lord goes even lower on the social scale from fishermen, choosing Levi Alpheus. This man, usually called Matthew, is a tax collector for the Roman government.

No patriotic, self-respecting Jew would be a tax collector. They were truly disgraceful, yet their corrupt methods made them wealthy. Nonetheless, Christ chooses Levi and attends his feast. In this way, the Lord gradually introduces the great truth that Israel needs a sacrifice for sin more than a conquering king. The religious leaders witnessing this are confused and offended. His announcement that he came to call sinners, not the righteous, was incomprehensible to them. To the Pharisees, only the righteous will have a place in the kingdom. Sinners will be destroyed in the judgments that precede it (Daniel 1:1–3).

3. Compare Daniel 12:3 to John 5:35. Who might Daniel be referring to when he mentions those who lead many to righteousness?

The Lord's words in Mark 2:17 are echoed in the story of the praying Pharisee and tax collector in Luke 18:9–14. There, the tax collector knows he is sick. The self-righteous Pharisee, however, is oblivious to his need for repentance.

Day Thirty-One

Mark 4:1–13

1 And he began again to teach by the sea side: and there was gathered unto him a great multitude, so that he entered into a ship, and sat in the sea; and the whole multitude was by the sea on the land.

2 And he taught them many things by parables, and said unto them in his doctrine,

3 Hearken; Behold, there went out a sower to sow:

4 And it came to pass, as he sowed, some fell by the way side, and the fowls of the air came and devoured it up.

5 And some fell on stony ground, where it had not much earth; and immediately it sprang up, because it had no depth of earth:

6 But when the sun was up, it was scorched; and because it had no root, it withered away.

7 And some fell among thorns, and the thorns grew up, and choked it, and it yielded no fruit.

8 And other fell on good ground, and did yield fruit that sprang up and increased; and brought forth, some thirty, and some sixty, and some an hundred.

9 And he said unto them, He that hath ears to hear, let him hear.

10 And when he was alone, they that were about him with the twelve asked of him the parable.

11 And he said unto them, Unto you it is given to know the mystery of the kingdom of God: but unto them that are without, all these things are done in parables:

12 That seeing they may see, and not perceive; and hearing they may hear, and not understand; lest at any time they should be converted, and their sins should be forgiven them.

13 And he said unto them, Know ye not this parable? and how then will ye know all parables?

A Resume of Christ's Work

The Lord's ministry makes a dramatic change in Mark 3. Jesus Christ ceases to preach the nearness of the kingdom and begins to use parables in speaking to the crowds. He does not do this to illustrate and simplify the truth. The parables are used to express the truth in veiled and obscure ways so that those who are not spiritual can never comprehend it (Matthew 13:10–13). Even his disciples could not understand his parables until he explained them.

1. Read Mark 4:12. Quoting Jeremiah 5:21, Christ gives his reason for speaking in parables. What is that reason?

The parable of the sower is a resume of Christ's ministry up to this time. He is the Sower. The wayside, the stony ground, the thorns and the good ground are the four groups in Israel who hear his word. The birds of the air, heat of the sun, and the choking thorns represent the usual trinity of evil—Satan, the flesh, and the world—that prevent the growth of the word. Only one small group, the Lord's disciples, is fruitful. A farmer would say that this is a very poor crop. This shows that the preaching of the kingdom has failed. Therefore, Christ takes a new direction in his ministry in preparation for his death.

2. 1 Corinthians 3:5–9 uses the image of sowing seeds. In verse 6, what causes the growth of the seeds?

The phrase, "He that hath ears to hear, let him hear" (Mark 4:9), is significant. Apparently, Jesus Christ is speaking to all people within range of his voice. But he uses images that can only be understood by those who have spiritual perception. The rest hear the sound but do not grasp the sense. Parables are puzzles that can be solved only by those who have the key.

3. Again, read Mark 4:11–12. In the last phrase of verse 12, what is another reason the Lord used parables?

It may seem shocking, but Jesus Christ did not use parables so that Israel could receive the pardon of sins. The very opposite was true. He spoke in parables so their sins would not be pardoned (Mark 4:12). The nation had rejected the gospel of the kingdom of the heavens and would soon murder their Messiah. The message from this time on is not gospel, but judgment. However, the kingdom gospel will be offered to Israel twice more—first in Acts, when it is again rejected, and finally at the end of this age, when Israel is saved (Romans 11:25–26; Revelation 7:10).

Today, we have the ministry of reconciliation (2 Corinthians 5:19). This is a very plainspoken ministry. We have no need to mask our message in parables. With the apostle Paul, "We entreat you on behalf of Christ, be reconciled to God" (2 Corinthians 5:20).

4. According to 2 Corinthians 5:19, what did God do in Christ?

DAY THIRTY-TWO

Mark 5:1–13

1 And they came over unto the other side of the sea, into the country of the Gadarenes.

2 And when he was come out of the ship, immediately there met him out of the tombs a man with an unclean spirit,

3 Who had his dwelling among the tombs; and no man could bind him, no, not with chains:

4 Because that he had been often bound with fetters and chains, and the chains had been plucked asunder by him, and the fetters broken in pieces: neither could any man tame him.

5 And always, night and day, he was in the mountains, and in the tombs, crying, and cutting himself with stones.

6 But when he saw Jesus afar off, he ran and worshipped him,

7 And cried with a loud voice, and said, What have I to do with thee, Jesus, thou Son of the most high God? I adjure thee by God, that thou torment me not.

8 For he said unto him, Come out of the man, thou unclean spirit.

9 And he asked him, What is thy name? And he answered, saying, My name is Legion: for we are many.

10 And he besought him much that he would not send them away out of the country.

11 Now there was there nigh unto the mountains a great herd of swine feeding.

12 And all the devils besought him, saying, Send us into the swine, that we may enter into them.

13 And forthwith Jesus gave them leave. And the unclean spirits went out, and entered into the swine: and the herd ran violently down a steep place into the sea, (they were about two thousand;) and were choked in the sea.

The Healing of Israel

The story of the Gadarene demoniac is told three times in the Gospels. It shows the fiercest display of the enemy's power entirely subjected to the Lord. Mark more fully describes the desperate condition of this man because his writing portrays Christ in service to humanity.

Here is a man possessed by so many demons that he is named Legion. A Roman legion was about six thousand strong. Strangely enough, these demons do not come out of him at the Lord's first command (Mark 5:8).

1. Read Isaiah 65:1–4. In verse 4, what are the similarities between Israel and the demoniac in Mark 5?

Before the Lord's arrival, the demoniac had been restless, rebellious, and self-abusive. This is remarkably similar to the history of Israel under the law. The chains and fetters of the law were never strong enough to hold them. Plus, they were often occupied with mad wars among themselves.

When God first sent his Son to the beloved nation, they would not be healed. Instead, they senselessly murdered their Messiah and his followers. Similarly, the Gadarene demoniac was not healed at the Lord's first command.

2. Matthew 12:43–45 describes Israel in the Lord's generation. What is their state after the Lord's first attempt to heal them?

Today's Israel has kept herself from idolatry for many centuries. But this will change at the end of this age when the great image is set up (Mark 13:14) and many worship the beast (Revelation 13:8). But just as the legion of demons is driven into the sea, Satan will be thrown into the abyss (20:1–3). What a change when the faithful of Israel, like the Gadarene demoniac, finds rest, righteousness, and reason at Christ's feet in the thousand years (v. 4).

3. In Revelation 13:8, certain people do not worship the beast because of Christ's sacrifice. Compare this verse with 1 Peter 1:19–20. When did God plan for Christ's death on the cross?

Day Thirty-Three

Mark 6:1–6

1 And he went out from thence, and came into his own country; and his disciples follow him.

2 And when the sabbath day was come, he began to teach in the synagogue: and many hearing him were astonished, saying, From whence hath this man these things? and what wisdom is this which is given unto him, that even such mighty works are wrought by his hands?

3 Is not this the carpenter, the son of Mary, the brother of James, and Joses, and of Juda, and Simon? and are not his sisters here with us? And they were offended at him.

4 But Jesus, said unto them, A prophet is not without honour, but in his own country, and among his own kin, and in his own house.

5 And he could there do no mighty work, save that he laid his hands upon a few sick folk, and healed them.

6 And he marvelled because of their unbelief. And he went round about the villages, teaching.

The Carpenter and the Tentmaker

Here, Jesus Christ returns to his hometown. The townsfolk have heard of his fame and marvel at his wisdom. Yet, they cannot bring themselves to believe that their townsman and relative could be sent from God. Still today, people who seek to speak the word of God routinely find their spiritual values discounted among their kindred.

1. Luke 4:16–30 tells of an earlier visit by the Lord to Nazareth. What was the townspeople's response to him at that time? (Read verse 29.)

2. In Psalm 69:7–8, why did Christ become a stranger to his kindred?

Jesus Christ was a carpenter (Mark 6:3). This shows a pleasant contrast between him and his apostle Paul:

- Jesus Christ was the servant of the Circumcision (Romans 15:8).

- Paul was his minister for the nations (v. 16).

- Christ was a carpenter who built permanent dwellings on earth. Similarly, Israel will dwell on the earth in the coming kingdom (Isaiah 60:21).

- Paul was a tentmaker. Those who believe under his ministry have no inheritance on earth. We are merely camping here, awaiting our heavenly dwelling place (1 Thessalonians 4:16–17).

When he spoke to the leaders of the church in Ephesus (Acts 20:34–35), Paul showed them his hands. "You know that I worked with these hands to provide my own needs and for those who were with me," he told them.

3. According to Matthew 15:24, to whom was Jesus Christ sent?

4. Read 1 Timothy 2:4, 7. What was one item that Paul was to teach to the Gentiles?

Like Paul, we do not know Christ according to the flesh (2 Corinthians 5:16). That is, we are not related to the Lord by physical ties as the Jewish people are. When we believed, we entered into a purely spiritual association with him. This is not on earth, but in the heavens (Ephesians 2:5–6).

Day Thirty-Four

Mark 7:1–8

1 Then came together unto him the Pharisees, and certain of the scribes, which came from Jerusalem.

2 And when they saw some of his disciples eat bread with defiled, that is to say, with unwashen, hands, they found fault.

3 For the Pharisees, and all the Jews, except they wash their hands oft, eat not, holding the tradition of the elders.

4 And when they come from the market, except they wash, they eat not. And many other things there be, which they have received to hold, as the washing of cups, and pots, brasen vessels, and of tables.

5 Then the Pharisees and scribes asked him, Why walk not thy disciples according to the tradition of the elders, but eat bread with unwashen hands?

6 He answered and said unto them, Well hath Esaias prophesied of you hypocrites, as it is written, This people honoureth me with their lips, but their heart is far from me.

7 Howbeit in vain do they worship me, teaching for doctrines the commandments of men.

8 For laying aside the commandment of God, ye hold the tradition of men, as the washing of pots and cups: and many other such like things ye do.

The Vanity of Tradition

It was the custom in Jesus' day to eat with the fingers. Yet, the Pharisees were not worried about cleanliness or table manners. They were worried about conformity to tradition, which had nothing to do with cleansing the inside of the hands that touched the food. They ceremonially rinsed the outside while clenching their fists when they washed.

1. The Pharisees were experts on the details of the Jewish traditions. Read Matthew 16:5–12. To what does Jesus liken the teachings of the Pharisees?

2. The Lord quotes Isaiah 29:13 in Mark 7:6. According to the verse in Isaiah, how does tradition influence worship?

Going to market involved contact with others (Mark 7:4), which the Pharisees considered contaminating. Afterward, they would not eat until they had been sprinkled with water. In the same way, the washing of cups, plates, and other vessels was not for cleanliness, but ceremonial purity. To the Pharisees, a token application of water in almost any way was considered highly devout.

Peter was probably one of the disciples eating without the ceremonial washing (Mark 7:5). He should have learned the lesson of the vanity of tradition. Later, after Christ's resurrection and ascension, Peter was sent to preach the gospel to a Gentile (Acts 10:1–48). Peter, like all the Jews, was so prejudiced against the Gentiles that it was almost impossible for him to conceive of such a thing, despite his learning firsthand from Jesus Christ about the emptiness of traditions. A voice had to speak to him in a vision three times, saying, "What God has made clean you must not call profane" (v. 15 NRSV).

3. Read Matthew 23:24–26. According to the Lord, what are people who follow tradition doing?

4. In 2 Timothy 3:5, how does Paul describe traditionalists?

Day Thirty-Five

Mark 9:14–29

14 And when he came to his disciples, he saw a great multitude about them, and the scribes questioning with them.

15 And straightway all the people, when they beheld him, were greatly amazed, and running to him saluted him.

16 And he asked the scribes, What question ye with them?

17 And one of the multitude answered and said, Master, I have brought unto thee my son, which hath a dumb spirit;

18 And wheresoever he taketh him, he teareth him: and he foameth, and gnasheth with his teeth, and pineth away: and I spake to thy disciples that they should cast him out; and they could not.

19 He answereth him, and saith, O faithless generation, how long shall I be with you? how long shall I suffer you? bring him unto me.

20 And they brought him unto him: and when he saw him, straightway the spirit tare him; and he fell on the ground, and wallowed foaming.

21 And he asked his father, How long is it ago since this came unto him? And he said, Of a child.

22 And ofttimes it hath cast him into the fire, and into the waters, to destroy him: but if thou canst do any thing, have compassion on us, and help us.

23 Jesus said unto him, If thou canst believe, all things are possible to him that believeth.

24 And straightway the father of the child cried out, and said with tears, Lord, I believe; help thou mine unbelief.

25 When Jesus saw that the people came running together, he rebuked the foul spirit, saying unto him, Thou dumb and deaf spirit, I charge thee, come out of him, and enter no more into him.

26 And the spirit cried, and rent him sore, and came out of him: and he was as one dead; insomuch that many said, He is dead.

27 But Jesus took him by the hand, and lifted him up; and he arose.

28 And when he was come into the house, his disciples asked him privately, Why could not we cast him out?

29 And he said unto them, This kind can come forth by nothing, but by prayer and fasting.

The Change in Christ's Ministry

Now, Jesus Christ descends from the mountain and begins his journey to the humiliation of Golgotha. His proclamation of the kingdom of the heavens has ended. The first symptom of this change is seen in that his disciples are unable to cast out a demon (Mark 9:18). It seems that the powers of darkness are aware of the change in Christ's ministry. He no longer displays his kingdom power; nor do his apostles. Instead, the Lord is laboring to teach a far more difficult lesson—his death and resurrection (Matthew 16:21). He does not want the disciples to proclaim the kingdom any longer (v. 20), so he withdraws their power over demons.

1. In Mark 9:24, a man prays, "Help my unbelief." According to Ephesians 2:8, what is the source of faith?

It is not that the disciples do not have enough faith to cast out the demon. Their problem is that they refuse to recognize the change in their master's ministry. Their ignorance is so great that Peter rebukes the Lord when he mentions his death and resurrection (Matthew 16:21–23).

2. According to Romans 8:7, where had Peter set his mind in the account of Matthew 16:21–23?

3. Romans 8:8 describes Peter in his refusal to accept the Lord's death and resurrection. What is this?

The significance of this story is seen in the ministry of the apostles in the book of Acts. Then, with the Lord's approval, they again preach the kingdom of the heavens to Israel. Like the demon in the boy, the beloved nation does not respond (Acts 4:1–22). The apostles' effort to bring the kingdom to Israel is a failure (28:25–28). But Christ will personally bring the kingdom to Israel, just as, after the apostles' failure, he healed the possessed boy (Mark 9:25; Zechariah 12:10).

4. Read Zechariah 12:10. What will God pour out on Israel when Christ comes again?

DAY THIRTY-SIX

Mark 10:17–31

17 And when he was gone forth into the way, there came one running, and kneeled to him, and asked him, Good Master, what shall I do that I may inherit eternal life? . . .

19 Thou knowest the commandments, Do not commit adultery, Do not kill, Do not steal, Do not bear false witness, Defraud not, Honour thy father and mother.

20 And he answered and said unto him, Master, all these have I observed from my youth.

21 Then Jesus beholding him loved him, and said unto him, One thing thou lackest: go thy way, sell whatsoever thou hast, and give to the poor, and thou shalt have treasure in heaven: and come, take up the cross, and follow me.

22 And he was sad at that saying, and went away grieved: for he had great possessions.

23 And Jesus looked round about, and saith unto his disciples, How hardly shall they that have riches enter into the kingdom of God!

24 And the disciples were astonished at his words. But Jesus answereth again, and saith unto them, Children, how hard is it for them that trust in riches to enter into the kingdom of God!

25 It is easier for a camel to go through the eye of a needle, than for a rich man to enter into the kingdom of God. . . .

28 Then Peter began to say unto him, Lo, we have left all, and have followed thee.

29 And Jesus answered and said, Verily I say unto you, There is no man that hath left house, or brethren, or sisters, or father, or mother, or wife, or children, or lands, for my sake, and the gospel's,

30 But he shall receive an hundredfold now in this time, houses, and brethren, and sisters, and mothers, and children, and lands, with persecutions; and in the world to come eternal life.

31 But many that are first shall be last; and the last first.

The Last Shall Be First

All nations reserve a high place for the wealthy. Such people have no difficulty in entering any establishment. Their wealth is the controlling factor in government. Policies are dictated, laws are passed, treaties are made, and wars are fought to protect invested capital and promote the increase of wealth. In God's kingdom, all this will be reversed (Mark 10:23–25). No rich man will enter it, because his riches will have been destroyed in judgment.

1. Read 1 Timothy 6:17–19. When a wealthy person is rich in good works, what is he actually doing? (See verse 19.)

In this present age of grace, many people have left all they have to follow the Lord but have not received hundred-fold what they have lost. This is because Mark 10:30 applies to the Jewish disciples when the kingdom was proclaimed in Israel. For example, after Pentecost, the disciples had all things in common. At that moment, each believer enjoyed hundreds of houses and fields (Acts 2:44–45; 4:32). The believers all cared for each other. No one was needy (4:34). Food was provided for everyone each day (6:1). This is not true today, notwithstanding our charity to the very poor. The believers at that time could do this because they were enjoying the benefits of citizenship in the kingdom of the heavens. This will again be true in the coming kingdom age.

2. In Acts 2:45, what did the believers do with the proceeds of the sales of their possessions?

3. Read Matthew 19:27–30. When will believers receive a hundred-fold of what they have left behind? (See verse 28.)

Those who gave up all their worldly possessions and expectations became the very poorest. They were the last that will become first in the kingdom (Mark 10:31). At that time, Peter honestly said, "I have no silver or gold " (Acts 3:6 NRSV). Yet, he forms a part of the foundation of the holy city, New Jerusalem (Revelation 21:14).

Day Thirty-Seven

Mark 11:1–11

1 And when they came nigh to Jerusalem, unto Bethphage and Bethany, at the mount of Olives, he sendeth forth two of his disciples,

2 And saith unto them, Go your way into the village over against you: and as soon as ye be entered into it, ye shall find a colt tied, whereon never man sat; loose him, and bring him.

3 And if any man say unto you, Why do ye this? say ye that the Lord hath need of him; and straightway he will send him hither.

4 And they went their way, and found the colt tied by the door without in a place where two ways met; and they loose him.

5 And certain of them that stood there said unto them, What do ye, loosing the colt?

6 And they said unto them even as Jesus had commanded: and they let them go.

7 And they brought the colt to Jesus, and cast their garments on him; and he sat upon him.

8 And many spread their garments in the way: and others cut down branches off the trees, and strawed them in the way.

9 And they that went before, and they that followed, cried, saying, Hosanna; Blessed is he that cometh in the name of the Lord:

10 Blessed be the kingdom of our father David, that cometh in the name of the Lord: Hosanna in the highest.

11 And Jesus entered into Jerusalem, and into the temple: and when he had looked round about upon all things, and now the eventide was come, he went out unto Bethany with the twelve.

The Last Visit to Jerusalem

The New Testament records only seven visits by Jesus Christ to Jerusalem. At those times, he actually visited the temple not the city itself. He came there only to fulfill the law and attend the festivals.

• During the first visit, he was dedicated to God as an infant (Luke 2:22).

- The second visit was when he was twelve years of age and found among the teachers in the temple (Luke 2:41–42).

- The third and fourth visits were for the Passover festivals at the beginning of his public ministry (John 2:13, 23).

- Next, he was in the temple for the festival of Tabernacles (John 7:2, 10) and festival of Dedications (10:22).

- The last occasion was again for the Passover festival (Mark 11:11), during which he was betrayed and crucified.

1. Read Exodus 12:1–13. What was the sacrifice in the first Passover?

2. In John 1:29, how does John the Baptist refer to Jesus Christ?

Mark shows Christ riding toward the city as the people honor him as king. "Blessed be the kingdom of our father David, that cometh in the name of the Lord," they shout (Mark 11:10). Yet, he does not immediately show himself in the palace of the king, but appears in the sanctuary of the temple. First, he must be the redeeming sacrifice before he can become the reigning king.

During this, his last visit to Jerusalem, Jesus not only visits the temple but is actually in the city itself: eating with his disciples in the upper room (Mark 14:15), in the house of the high priest (Matthew 26:57), in the palace of the governor (27:1–2), and in Herod's quarters (Luke 23:6–7). At his first visit, a sacrifice was offered for him (Luke 2:24). At the last visit, the Lord himself is the sacrifice.

3. In John 12:49–53, what is the high priest's prophesy about Christ's death?

Day Thirty-Eight

Mark 12:1–12

1 And he began to speak unto them by parables. A certain man planted a vineyard, and set an hedge about it, and digged a place for the winefat, and built a tower, and let it out to husbandmen, and went into a far country.

2 And at the season he sent to the husbandmen a servant, that he might receive from the husbandmen of the fruit of the vineyard.

3 And they caught him, and beat him, and sent him away empty.

4 And again he sent unto them another servant; and at him they cast stones, and wounded him in the head, and sent him away shamefully handled.

5 And again he sent another; and him they killed, and many others; beating some, and killing some.

6 Having yet therefore one son, his wellbeloved, he sent him also last unto them, saying, They will reverence my son.

7 But those husbandmen said among themselves, This is the heir; come, let us kill him, and the inheritance shall be ours.'

8 And they took him, and killed him, and cast him out of the vineyard.

9 What shall therefore the lord of the vineyard do? he will come and destroy the husbandmen, and will give the vineyard unto others.

10 And have ye not read this scripture; The stone which the builders rejected is become the head of the corner:

11 This was the Lord's doing, and it is marvellous in our eyes?

12 And they sought to lay hold on him, but feared the people: for they knew that he had spoken the parable against them: and they left him, and went their way.

The Rejected Cornerstone

Vineyards were quite familiar to those who heard this parable. In those days, stones were built into broad fences around the vines. The vat in which the grapes were pressed was dug out of the natural rock. When the grapes were ripe, a guard watched over them from a tower that overlooked the whole vineyard.

Israel is the vineyard of Jehovah (Isaiah 5:7). The parable of the vineyard describes the way the nation treated God's messengers and prophets. This is one long story of rebellion and violence that came to its climax in the death of the Son of God. Israel's priests, scribes, and elders are the farmers responsible for the vineyard. In this story, the Lord reminds them that they not only killed the prophets that had come before, but they would soon kill him, their Messiah.

1. In Mark 11:28, what do the priests, scribes, and elders ask that is answered in the parable of the vineyard?

Israel's leaders are simply hired hands. They have no authority over God's people when the Son of God is on the scene. The vineyard belongs to his Father so they are answerable to him. Though this is a parable, they know the Lord is speaking of them, predicting the rejection of his authority and their murder of him (Mark 12:12). Yet, they persist in their program of putting him to death in spite of this preview of their crime, proving the utter depravity of their priesthood. They will have no place in the kingdom (v. 9). The twelve apostles under the authority of Christ will replace their rule.

2. Read Isaiah 5:1–6. What did God do to his fruitless vineyard?

The Lord's final word to his questioners is a quote from Psalm 118 (vv. 22–23): "The stone which the builders rejected is become the head of the corner" (Mark 12:10). The priests, scribes, and elders know these verses well. They also know that a building's cornerstone is the most beautiful. But they refuse to give Christ any place in Israel much less the chief place he deserves. They do not join the psalmist in singing, "This is the day that the Lord has made; let us rejoice and be glad in it" (Psalm 118:24 NRSV). Instead, they reject and despise him.

3. Read 1 Peter 2:4–8. Why did Israel stumble over the cornerstone? (See verse 8.)

No doubt, Peter is present to witness the Lord's scathing testimony to the leaders of Israel. Not long after this, these same priests, elders, and scribes question Peter's authority just as they did his Master's (Acts 4:5–7). He takes this opportunity to confirm the message of the parable of the vineyard:

> Then Peter, filled with the Holy Spirit, said to them: "Rulers and elders of the people! If we are being called to account today for an act of kindness shown to a cripple and are asked how he was healed, then know this, you and all the people of Israel: It is by the name of Jesus Christ of Nazareth, whom you crucified but whom God raised from the dead, that this man stands before you healed. He is 'the stone you builders rejected, which has become the capstone'" (Acts 4:8–11 NIV).

4. According to Isaiah 28:16, what is the benefit in trusting the precious cornerstone?

Day Thirty-Nine

Mark 14:1–10

1 After two days was the feast of the passover, and of unleavened bread: and the chief priests and the scribes sought how they might take him by craft, and put him to death.

2 But they said, Not on the feast day, lest there be an uproar of the people.

3 And being in Bethany in the house of Simon the leper, as he sat at meat, there came a woman having an alabaster box of ointment of spikenard very precious; and she brake the box, and poured it on his head.

4 And there were some that had indignation within themselves, and said, Why was this waste of the ointment made?

5 For it might have been sold for more than three hundred pence, and have been given to the poor. And they murmured against her.

6 And Jesus said, Let her alone; why trouble ye her? she hath wrought a good work on me.

7 For ye have the poor with you always, and whensoever ye will ye may do them good: but me ye have not always.

8 She hath done what she could: she is come aforehand to anoint my body to the burying.

9 Verily I say unto you, Wheresoever this gospel shall be preached throughout the whole world, this also that she hath done shall be spoken of for a memorial of her.

10 And Judas Iscariot, one of the twelve, went unto the chief priests, to betray him unto them.

A Woman's Wasteful Worship

The Lord was anointed twice during the last week of his life. First, six days before the Passover a woman anointed his feet (Luke 7:36–38). Here, a woman pours the ointment on Christ's head. This occurs in connection with his entrance into Jerusalem as the king. When a king was crowned in Israel, he was anointed with oil (1 Samuel 10:1).

1. In Luke 7:38, what five things did the woman do while worshiping the Lord?

The Messiah comes to Jerusalem, the city of the great king (Psalm 48:2), but no one thinks of anointing him. His disciples are even resentful of this as it takes place (Mark 14:4–5). They are miserly with the price of the oil for the anointing of their Messiah! Yet, this unnamed woman gives him the honor he deserves. Characteristically, Jesus Christ does not emphasize his kingship as this happens. Instead, he points to his sacrifice (v. 8). This is in keeping with Mark's depiction of him as a servant.

This story shows a woman in intelligent, sacrificial worship. She alone, of all his followers, seems to understand that he is about to die. Only she appreciates the preciousness of this death. Her time, effort, and treasure are wasted in worship. This gains Christ's gratitude and touches his heart.

2. Read John 19:38–40. How many pounds of spices do Joseph of Arimathea and Nicodemus bring to prepare Jesus' body *after* his death?

Spiritual worship heaps all on Christ Jesus. The most generous of philanthropists cannot hold company with this woman. Yet, she simply did what she could with what she had—an example to us all. This nameless woman sacrificed for Jesus Christ while Judas profited from him. He contracted with the chief priests to betray the Lord. They rejoiced (v. 11) and promised Judas thirty pieces of silver (Matthew 26:15).

3. In Exodus 21:32, what is the value of a slave? Compare this with Matthew 26:15.

Day Forty

Mark 15:1–15

1 And straightway in the morning the chief priests held a consultation with the elders and scribes and the whole council, and bound Jesus, and carried him away, and delivered him to Pilate.

2 And Pilate asked him, Art thou the King of the Jews? And he answering said unto them, Thou sayest it.

3 And the chief priests accused him of many things: but he answered nothing.

4 And Pilate asked him again, saying, Answerest thou nothing? behold how many things they witness against thee.

5 But Jesus yet answered nothing; so that Pilate marvelled.

6 Now at that feast he released unto them one prisoner, whomsoever they desired.

7 And there was one named Barabbas, which lay bound with them that had made insurrection with him, who had committed murder in the insurrection.

8 And the multitude crying aloud began to desire him to do as he had ever done unto them.

9 But Pilate answered them, saying, Will ye that I release unto you the King of the Jews?

10 For he knew that the chief priests had delivered him for envy.

11 But the chief priests moved the people, that he should rather release Barabbas unto them.

12 And Pilate answered and said again unto them, What will ye then that I shall do unto him whom ye call the King of the Jews?

13 And they cried out again, Crucify him.

14 Then Pilate said unto them, Why, what evil hath he done? And they cried out the more exceedingly, Crucify him.

15 And so Pilate, willing to content the people, released Barabbas unto them, and delivered Jesus, when he had scourged him, to be crucified.

The Trial of Jesus Christ

The Sanhedrin were Israel's supreme counsel. They had jurisdiction in religious affairs but could not rule that an offender deserved death. Only the civil authorities of Rome made this judgment (John 18:31). This is why the Jewish leaders had to get Pilate's ruling in order to have Jesus Christ executed.

1. In Acts 6:8–7:60, the Jewish Sanhedrin judges Stephen. What does the counsel do that is illegal according to John 18:31? (See vv. 58–60.)

2. In Acts 22:30–23:12, Paul has a hearing before the Sanhedrin. In 23:12–15, what agreement does the counsel enter into?

Pilate, the Roman governor, is not interested in the Jew's religious differences. His concern is to guard the state. This is why he first asks the Lord Jesus, "Art thou the King of the Jews?" (Mark 15:2). If this were true, Christ would be a threat to the authority of Rome. The Lord does not deny that he is a king. However, he explains to Pilate that at that time his kingdom is not of this world, and that his followers will not fight (John 18:36). This is all Pilate needs to know. If Christ is not planning violence, he is no menace to the Roman power.

3. According to John 19:11, from where did Pilate obtain his power?

Though ignorant of scripture, Pilate was impressed by the claims of Christ and tried to release him. In contrast, the priests had devoted their lives to the study of God's law. Yet, they were blind to the clear testimony of their Messiah. Even though they had no ears to hear his words, they should have heeded the Lord's silence (Mark 15:5) because it was foretold in their scriptures: "He was oppressed and afflicted, yet he did not open his mouth; he was led like a lamb to the slaughter, and as a sheep before her shearers is silent, so he did not open his mouth" (Isaiah 53:7 NIV).

DAY FORTY-ONE

Mark 16:10–20

10 And she went and told them that had been with him, as they mourned and wept.

11 And they, when they had heard that he was alive, and had been seen of her, believed not.

12 After that he appeared in another form unto two of them, as they walked, and went into the country.

13 And they went and told it unto the residue: neither believed they them.

14 Afterward he appeared unto the eleven as they sat at meat, and upbraided them with their unbelief and hardness of heart, because they believed not them which had seen him after he was risen.

15 And he said unto them, Go ye into all the world, and preach the gospel to every creature.

16 He that believeth and is baptized shall be saved; but he that believeth not shall be damned.

17 And these signs shall follow them that believe; In my name shall they cast out devils; they shall speak with new tongues;

18 They shall take up serpents; and if they drink any deadly thing, it shall not hurt them; they shall lay hands on the sick, and they shall recover.

19 So then after the Lord had spoken unto them, he was received up into heaven, and sat on the right hand of God.

20 And they went forth, and preached every where, the Lord working with them, and confirming the word with signs following. Amen.

The Gospel to All Creation

Some of the most ancient authorities end the book of Mark at verse 8. However, most authorities include verses 9–20 immediately after verse 8, though some of them mark the passage as doubtful. The reason for this confusion is a failure to understand the proper place of the Lord's commission to the eleven apostles (Mark 16:15–18).

1. In Mark 16:15, where are the apostles to go, and what are they to do?

2. What are the five signs that will accompany those who believe under Mark's commission? (See verses 17–18.)

Those who originally tried to fulfill this commission found they could not cast out demons, handle deadly serpents, drink poison, or raise the dead. They may, however, have seemingly had success in speaking new languages or helping the sick. Plus, this commission is for *all creation*. It is not confined to Israel, the nations, or even all mankind, but includes the entire realm of creation—an impossible field to evangelize in this age.

Paul, in his earlier ministries, has a part in this commission. While on the island of Melita, a viper fastens on his hand. The natives look for him to fall dead, but he shakes it off into the fire with no ill effects (Acts 28:1–6). There he heals the father of the headman of the island and many others (vv. 7–9). This shows that the kingdom, with its accompanying powers, arrived on Melita when Paul was shipwrecked there.

Mark's creation commission now awaits its fulfillment when the kingdom fully comes (Revelation 11:15). Then its signs reverse the curse of Eden in casting out the powers of darkness, communication with the lower creatures, neutralizing the poison of sin, and general healing.

3. Read Revelation 20:2. What part of Mark's commission is fulfilled here?

Day Forty-Two

Acts 12:11–12
And when Peter was come to himself. . .he came to the house of Mary the mother of John, whose surname was Mark; where many were gathered together praying.

1 Peter 5:13
The church that is at Babylon, elected together with you, saluteth you; and so doth Marcus my son.

Mark 14:51
And there followed him a certain young man, having a linen cloth cast about his naked body; and the young men laid hold on him: And he left the linen cloth, and fled from them naked.

Acts 12:25
And Barnabas and Saul returned from Jerusalem, when they had fulfilled their ministry, and took with them John, whose surname was Mark.

Acts 13:5, 13
And when they were at Salamis, they preached the word of God in the synagogues of the Jews: and they had also John to their minister. . . . Now when Paul and his company loosed from Paphos, they came to Perga in Pamphylia: and John departing from them returned to Jerusalem.

Acts 15:36–39
And some days after Paul said unto Barnabas, Let us go again and visit our brethren in every city. . .and see how they do. And Barnabas determined to take with them John, whose surname was Mark. But Paul thought not good to take him with them, who departed from them from Pamphylia. . . . And the contention was so sharp between them, that they departed asunder one from the other: and so Barnabas took Mark, and sailed unto Cyprus.

Colossians 4:10–11

Aristarchus my fellow prisoner saluteth you, and Marcus, sister's son to Barnabas, (touching whom ye received commandments: if he come unto you, receive him;) And Jesus, which is called Justus, who are of the circumcision. These only are my fellow workers unto the kingdom of God, which have been a comfort unto me.

2 Timothy 4:11

Only Luke is with me. Take Mark, and bring him with thee: for he is profitable to me for the ministry.

The Ministry of Mark

It is supposed that John Mark is the writer of this book. If this is so, it is a striking instance of God's grace and wisdom. As a servant, Mark was a notable failure among Christ's followers, yet he wrote the story of the perfect servant.

Mark was the son of a godly mother in whose home the disciples met for worship and prayer (Acts 12:12). He was the cousin of Barnabas (Colossians 4:10) and probably a convert of Peter (1 Peter 5:13). Some say that it was Mark who ran naked from the scene of Jesus Christ's arrest (Mark 14:51). If so, this event provides an insight into the man. He was wearing only a linen cloth that night. In the scriptures, linen clothing represents righteousness. Yet, the conduct of Mark and the other disciples as Christ was betrayed and arrested exposed their shame and total lack of righteousness.

1. Read Revelation 19:8. The bride of the Lamb is wearing fine linen, bright and pure. What does this clothing represent?

Barnabas and Paul brought Mark with them to Antioch from Jerusalem (Acts 12:25). He was chosen to accompany the two apostles on their first missionary journey (Acts 13:5), yet he deserted them at Perga and returned to Jerusalem (v. 13). The reason for this may have been that Mark, a Jew from Jerusalem, was offended that Paul preached the gospel to the Gentile ruler in Paphos (vv. 7, 12). Barnabas wanted to take Mark on their second journey, but Paul would not have it and rather than take Mark along, separated from Barnabas (Acts 15:36–39).

As always, God uses failure to advance the purpose of the ages. Mark's failure was used by God to separate Paul from direct links with Jerusalem. He no longer worked with Barnabas, who early on was among the disciples in Jerusalem (Acts 4:36). Instead, he traveled with Silas who was from the church in Antioch (15:32). This severing from Jerusalem was necessary for the good news to reach the Gentiles.

2. In 2 Corinthians 12:7–10, Paul talks about his weakness. How did God use this for good?

3. Read Galatians 2:7–8. Who was entrusted with the gospel to the circumcision (Israel)? Who was given the gospel for the uncircumcised (the Gentiles)?

After deserting the apostle in Perga, Mark somehow discovers the blessings of grace. From Perga he had retreated to Jerusalem to be among the multitudes of Jewish believers who were zealous for the law (Acts 21:20). But when he appears again in the divine story, Mark is recommended to the Gentile church in Colossi (Colossians 4:10). By then, he, Aristarchus, and Justus are the only Jews among Paul's co-workers (v. 11). He clearly is no longer prejudiced against the Gentiles. To Paul, Mark is "useful for the service". (2 Timothy 4:11).

Mark presents us with Jesus Christ as the servant of the circumcision (Romans 15:8). Jesus never leaves the land. He does not give the children of Israel's bread to Gentile dogs (Mark 7:27). Very few crumbs fall from the table to feed those outside the tiny land of Israel. And yet, through Israel, after his resurrection, Christ Jesus reaches out with blessing for the whole creation (16:15).

4. In Romans 15:8, why is Christ the servant of the circumcision?

Answer Key to Questions in Mark

Day Question

29. 1. Mary, pregnant with Jesus Christ, entered Zechariah's house where Elizabeth was pregnant with John.
    2. Grace and truth.
    3. Christ Jesus came to save the world.

30. 1. They were amazed and glorified God.
    2. The Lord does not remember sins.
    3. John the Baptist.

31. 1. Seeing they do not see and hearing they do not hear.
    2. God gives the growth.
    3. So that they may not turn again and be forgiven.
    4. God reconciled the world to himself.

32. 1. They live in tombs and eat swine's flesh.
    2. Their last state was worse than the first.
    3. Before the foundation of the earth.

33. 1. They drove him out of town and tried to throw him off a cliff.
    2. For God's sake.
    3. The lost sheep of the house of Israel.
    4. God desires everyone to be saved and to come to the knowledge of the truth.

34. 1. Leaven.
    2. Worship becomes a human commandment learned by rote.
    3. They strain at a gnat and swallow a camel.
    4. They have the form of godliness, but they deny its power.

35. 1. It is a gift of God.
    2. He had set his mind on the flesh.
    3. He was hostile to God.
    4. The spirit of grace and of supplications.

36. 1. They are laying hold of the life that is really life (1 Timothy 6:19).
    2. They distributed the proceeds to all who had need.
    3. When the Son of Man is seated on the throne of his glory in the coming kingdom.

37. 1. A lamb for each household.
    2. "Here is the Lamb of God who takes away the sin of the world."
    3. Jesus was to die for the nation of Israel.

38. 1. "By what authority are you doing these things?"
    2. God made the vineyard a waste.
    3. Because they disobeyed the word, as they were destined to do.
    4. The person who trusts will never be dismayed (NIV).

39. 1. She wept, bathed his feet with her tears, dried them with her hair, kissed his feet, and anointed them with the ointment.
    2. One hundred pounds.
    3. Thirty shekels of silver.

40. 1. They put Stephen to death.
    2. They join a conspiracy to assassinate Paul.
    3. God gave Pilate his power.

41. 1. They are to go into the entire world and proclaim the good news to the whole creation.
    2. Cast out demons in the Lord's name, speak in new languages, pick up snakes, be unhurt by poisons, heal the sick.
    3. The power behind the demons is cast out.

42. 1. The righteous deeds of the saints.
    2. God's strength is made perfect in weakness.
    3. Peter was the apostle to the Jews. Paul was the apostle to the nations.
    4. For the sake of the truth of God and to confirm the promises God made to Israel's patriarchs.

Introduction to
the Gospel of Luke

A vast range of human sympathy is found in Luke's account of the Lord's life. Its genealogy shows this (Luke 3:23–38). He is the true man; the Son of Man who came to seek and to save that which Adam lost. He will completely undo the effects of Adam's sin and restore to humanity all that he forfeited.

Luke shows that repentance and remission of sins are not Israel's alone. These are to be preached to the whole human race, beginning at Jerusalem (Luke 24:47). As promised, all the nations will be blessed through Israel. Luke's other book in the New Testament, Acts, depicts the further advance of this commission (Acts 1:8). It shows that from Jerusalem, the message spread to all Judea and to Samaria. After this, the apostle Paul took it to the nations in his early ministry.

Luke is the longest account of the Lord's life. It records six miracles and eleven parables that are not found elsewhere. Each of these characterizes Christ as the sympathetic Savior and healer of his people. The miraculous catch of fish makes Peter a fisher of men (5:4–11). The raising of the widow's son restores him to his grieving mother (7:11–18). The woman with a crippling spirit is released (13:11–13). The man with edema is healed on the Sabbath (14:1–6). Ten lepers are cleansed, but only the Samaritan thanks him (17:12–19). A slave has his ear cut off and, in the midst of his arrest, Christ heals it. Such scenes of sympathy and salvation pervade this portrayal of our Lord.

Like the other gospels, Luke's account hinges on Israel's blessing. But God's favored nation rejected the Son of God and his ministry. So, they are put to one side aside for the time being. The completion of Israel's commission must wait until the nation is restored to God's favor (Romans 11:15).

Day Forty-Three

Luke 1:39–56

39 And Mary arose in those days, and went into the hill country with haste, into a city of Judah;

40 And entered into the house of Zacharias, and saluted Elisabeth.

41 And it came to pass, that, when Elisabeth heard the salutation of Mary, the babe leaped in her womb; and Elisabeth was filled with the Holy Ghost:

42 And she spake out with a loud voice, and said, Blessed art thou among women, and blessed is the fruit of thy womb.

43 And whence is this to me, that the mother of my Lord should come to me?

44 For, lo, as soon as the voice of thy salutation sounded in mine ears, the babe leaped in my womb for joy.

45 And blessed is she that believed: for there shall be a performance of those things which were told her from the Lord.

46 And Mary said, My soul doth magnify the Lord,

47 And my spirit hath rejoiced in God my Saviour.

48 For he hath regarded the low estate of his handmaiden: for, behold, from henceforth all generations shall call me blessed.

49 For he that is mighty hath done to me great things; and holy is his name.

50 And his mercy is on them that fear him from generation to generation.

51 He hath shewed strength with his arm; he hath scattered the proud in the imagination of their hearts.

52 He hath put down the mighty from their seats, and exalted them of low degree.

53 He hath filled the hungry with good things; and the rich he hath sent empty away.

54 He hath helped his servant Israel, in remembrance of his mercy;

55 As he spake to our fathers, to Abraham, and to his seed for ever.

56 And Mary abode with her about three months, and returned to her own house.

Mary's Prophecy

John the Baptist came to prepare the way for Jesus Christ, and he does this even before he is born. Mary kept the secret of the Messiah's birth to herself. She trusted God to make it known in his own time. Yet, the very moment she comes into the presence of the unborn John, he recognizes his Lord and rejoices in his presence (Luke 1:41, 44). The angel Gabriel had told her of Elizabeth's pregnancy, and Elizabeth's words reveal that she knows of Mary's condition (vv. 41–45). All this has a wonderful effect on Mary.

1. Compare Isaiah 40:3 and Luke 3:4. What was John the Baptist sent to do?

The joy and exultation of these women give us a foretaste of the effect of the coming of Christ. Beginning with two Jewish mothers—one quite young, the other very old—in an obscure Judean village, its widening circle includes:

- The early followers of Jesus Christ (Acts 2:1–4).

- Then the whole nation of Israel (Romans 11:26).

- Through Israel, all the nations of the earth are blessed in the kingdom of the heavens (Genesis 26:4; Revelation 11:15).

- In the present day, before the kingdom comes, the gospel has delivered heavenly blessings to the nations (Ephesians 1:3) despite the stumbling of Israel (Romans 11:11).

With the words "Blessed art thou among women, and blessed is the fruit of thy womb" (Luke 1:42), Elizabeth begins the song that swells into the anthem of the entire universe at the consummation when God becomes all in all (1 Corinthians 15:28).

Mary's response is simple and uplifting. The lyrical beauty and prophetic power of its seven-fold praise place this girl among the greatest of Israel's prophets:

- Those who magnify the Lord cannot help but be happy (Luke 1:46–47).

- She, a lowly slave, becomes the most blessed of all generations (v. 48).

- Those who humble themselves are sure to be blessed (v. 49–50).

- She is proof that God will scatter the proud and exalt the low (vv. 51–52).

- The hungry will be filled and the rich emptied.

- God will visit downtrodden Israel and place them on the throne (v. 54).

- God will perform all the promises made to Abraham and the prophets (v. 55).

> 2. Mary's case proves the truth of 1 Corinthians 1:20. What is that truth?

> 3. Read Genesis 22:17–18. What are the promises God made to Abraham?

Mary proclaims that, in the conception of Christ in her womb, God "has helped his servant Israel. . .according to the promise he made to our ancestors" (Luke 1:54–55 NRSV). Micah 7:18–20 (NIV) is a beautiful example of God's promises to Israel that are fulfilled in the coming of Jesus Christ:

Who is a God like you,
    who pardons sin and forgives the transgression
    of the remnant of his inheritance?
You do not stay angry forever but delight to show mercy.
You will again have compassion on us;
    you will tread our sins underfoot
    and hurl all our iniquities into the depths of the sea.
You will be true to Jacob,
    and show mercy to Abraham,
    as you pledged on oath to our fathers in days long ago.

Day Forty-Four

Luke 2:41–52

41 Now his parents went to Jerusalem every year at the feast of the passover.

42 And when he was twelve years old, they went up to Jerusalem after the custom of the feast.

43 And when they had fulfilled the days, as they returned, the child Jesus tarried behind in Jerusalem; and Joseph and his mother knew not of it.

44 But they, supposing him to have been in the company, went a day's journey; and they sought him among their kinsfolk and acquaintance.

45 And when they found him not, they turned back again to Jerusalem, seeking him.

46 And it came to pass, that after three days they found him in the temple, sitting in the midst of the doctors, both hearing them, and asking them questions.

47 And all that heard him were astonished at his understanding and answers.

48 And when they saw him, they were amazed: and his mother said unto him, Son, why hast thou thus dealt with us? behold, thy father and I have sought thee sorrowing.

49 And he said unto them, How is it that ye sought me? wist ye not that I must be about my Father's business?

50 And they understood not the saying which he spake unto them.

51 And he went down with them, and came to Nazareth, and was subject unto them: but his mother kept all these sayings in her heart.

52 And Jesus increased in wisdom and stature, and in favour with God and man.

Christ Prepares for His Ministry

A Jewish boy was not expected to attend the Passover in Jerusalem until he was twelve years of age. At that age, he was answerable for his acts and responsible to keep the festival and relate to the law as an individual. This is why Jesus Christ goes with his parents to Jerusalem. While there, he acts independently of them by associating with the teachers of the law in the temple and does not return with them after the seven days of the festival are over. He is free to prepare for his future ministry. This begins the separation that will bring him entirely into the work and under the will of God.

1. Isaiah 11:1–4 describes Christ. What three aspects of the Spirit did the Lord display to the teachers in the temple? (See verse 2.)

2. In Matthew 2:13–15, what did Joseph do to protect the child Jesus from danger?

By this time, Herod is dead and Archelaus banished (Matthew 2:20–22). Nonetheless, the boy is not among those returning to Galilee from the festival. So, Mary and Joseph no doubt relive the dread inspired by the massacre of the little boys in Bethlehem (Matthew 2:16–18). They know that Christ's royal rights could endanger his life. In their minds, it is possible that he is not simply lost among the thousands who crowd the roads out of the holy city.

3. Read Luke 2:34. What did Simeon tell Mary that could have fed her anxiety when Jesus went missing?

Christ's astonishing discussion with the teachers in the temple drew attention to the boy. Couldn't someone have been reminded of the phenomena and predictions that accompanied his infancy? No wonder his mother scolds, "Child, why have you treated us like this? Look, your father and I have been searching for you in great anxiety" (Luke 2:48 NRSV).

Day Forty-Five

Luke 4:1–13

1 And Jesus being full of the Holy Ghost returned from Jordan, and was led by the Spirit into the wilderness,

2 Being forty days tempted of the devil. And in those days he did eat nothing: and when they were ended, he afterward hungered.

3 And the devil said unto him, If thou be the Son of God, command this stone that it be made bread.

4 And Jesus answered him, saying, It is written, That man shall not live by bread alone, but by every word of God.

5 And the devil, taking him up into an high mountain, shewed unto him all the kingdoms of the world in a moment of time.

6 And the devil said unto him, All this power will I give thee, and the glory of them: for that is delivered unto me; and to whomsoever I will I give it.

7 If thou therefore wilt worship me, all shall be thine.

8 And Jesus answered and said unto him, Get thee behind me, Satan: for it is written, Thou shalt worship the Lord thy God, and him only shalt thou serve.

9 And he brought him to Jerusalem, and set him on a pinnacle of the temple, and said unto him, If thou be the Son of God, cast thyself down from hence:

10 For it is written, He shall give his angels charge over thee, to keep thee:

11 And in their hands they shall bear thee up, lest at any time thou dash thy foot against a stone.

12 And Jesus answering said unto him, It is said, Thou shalt not tempt the Lord thy God.

13 And when the devil had ended all the temptation, he departed from him for a season.

The Three-Fold Temptation of Christ

"And so it is written, the first man Adam was made a living soul; the last Adam was made a quickening spirit" (1 Corinthians 15:45 NIV).

The first Adam's dominant aspect was soul. That of the last Adam, Jesus Christ, is spirit. This is clearly seen in the ways they responded to the tempter. The first man, Adam, failed on every point. The second man, Christ, was tempted many times more severely, yet stood the test triumphantly.

- Adam was in no need of food, yet he sinned (Genesis 3:6).

- Christ was famished from a forty-day fast yet withstood the temptation of food (Luke 4:1–4).

- Adam was in a beautiful garden and was the head of all creatures on earth, yet he yielded to Satan (Genesis 2:28–30).

- Christ was in a wilderness among wild beasts yet refused to trade worship for the headship that was rightfully his (Luke 4:5–7).

- Adam questioned God's goodness and sinned by grasping that which God withheld (Genesis 3:4–5).

- Christ refused to doubt God's love and would not put it to a test (Luke 4:12).

   1. In both Luke 4:4 and 8, Jesus Christ responded to the devil in the same way. What is this?

Christ is to be the king of Israel. So, he must overcome the opposition of men. But before he can do this, he must conquer the spirit that operates in them (Ephesians 2:2) and rules the darkness of this world (6:12). This is Satan, who took authority away from mankind through his deception in the garden (1 Timothy 2:14).

Christ is tempted in three ways and overcomes God's enemy each time: first in his body, second in his spirit, and third in his soul. The first involves his using miraculous powers to feed himself (Luke 4:3). He refuses this, countering the temptation with the Word of God. His choice is to depend only on God.

   2. Read Deuteronomy 8:3. How did God help Israel understand that "man does not live on bread alone but on every word that comes from the mouth of the Lord" (NIV)?

Secondly, Christ is offered the rule of the world in trade for his worship of Satan (Luke 4:5–8). But he knows that the throne of the kingdom is already his (Daniel 7:13–14) and refuses to avoid the suffering and shame that lie between him and that throne by accepting the kingdom from the Slanderer. Again, Christ reminds his enemy, "It is written," and the word of God silences the enemy.

3. In Luke 16:13, what happens when someone tries to worship two gods?

Finally, the devil turns the Lord's method back on him, quoting the Bible in temptation (Luke 4:10). But the Lord trumps this, quoting the law—"Do not put the Lord your God to the test" (Deuteronomy 6:16 NRSV).

4. In Numbers 21:4–6, Israel tests God. What happened to them? (See 1 Corinthians 10:9).

One day the Lamb will defeat the Dragon in the end of this age (Revelation 20:2). Here, the Dove meets the Serpent in the wilderness and conquers it (Luke 3:25). Physically, Christ showed unreserved dependence on God's provision (Luke 4:4); in his spirit, he was centered on God's service (v. 8), and his soul was full of trust in God's faithfulness (v. 12). These are more than a match for the Slanderer.

DAY FORTY-SIX

Luke 5:1–11

1 And it came to pass, that, as the people pressed upon him to hear the word of God, he stood by the lake of Gennesaret,

2 And saw two ships standing by the lake: but the fishermen were gone out of them, and were washing their nets.

3 And he entered into one of the ships, which was Simon's, and prayed him that he would thrust out a little from the land. And he sat down, and taught the people out of the ship.

4 Now when he had left speaking, he said unto Simon, Launch out into the deep, and let down your nets for a draught.

5 And Simon answering said unto him, Master, we have toiled all the night, and have taken nothing: nevertheless at thy word I will let down the net.

6 And when they had this done, they inclosed a great multitude of fishes: and their net brake.

7 And they beckoned unto their partners, which were in the other ship, that they should come and help them. And they came, and filled both the ships, so that they began to sink.

8 When Simon Peter saw it, he fell down at Jesus' knees, saying, Depart from me; for I am a sinful man, O Lord.

9 For he was astonished, and all that were with him, at the draught of the fishes which they had taken:

10 And so was also James, and John, the sons of Zebedee, which were partners with Simon. And Jesus said unto Simon, Fear not; from henceforth thou shalt catch men.

11 And when they had brought their ships to land, they forsook all, and followed him.

Christ the Fisherman

Three principal methods of fishing are referenced in the scriptures. Peter caught the fish that had the temple-tax money in its mouth with a hook and line (Matthew 17:27). Matthew 13:47 mentions a seine or dragnet that was played out from a boat and dragged to the shore

(13:47–48). Smaller nets were cast from boats in nighttime fishing (John 21:3). It was considered foolish to even attempt to net-fish in the daytime. This is the method Jesus suggests when Simon Peter mildly protests the idea (Luke 5:5). If they cannot catch any fish at night, why even try in broad daylight?

1. This is the second time the Lord calls these fishermen. Matthew 4:18–22 records the first occasion. Whom did he call at that time?

2. In Matthew 4:19, how did Christ describe the disciples' new occupation?

Peter does as he is told without the least expectation of results. It is difficult to imagine the awe and dismay of these professional fishermen when their catch is enormous. To fill two boats with a single catch would be a miracle, even at night. They do not yet know that the man who told them to do it is the most remarkable fisherman who ever lived!

3. When Christ resurrected, he again instructed Peter and the others how to fish (John 21:4–14). How many large fish did they catch? (See verse 11.)

This miracle describes the ministry of Jesus Christ and portrays him as the great fisher of men. The fish represent the disciples that he caught as he proclaimed the kingdom in Israel. The broken net sadly pictures his sufferings for them. Peter, James, and John salvage the fish, but their boats are swamped. This signifies their ministries in the era following Christ's death. Though they labored well, Israel rejected the kingdom (Acts 12:1–3; 21:20; 28:28).

4. When Christ is in resurrection, does the net break (John 21:7–11)?

Day Forty-Seven

Luke 6:1–11

1 And it came to pass on the second sabbath after the first, that he went through the corn fields; and his disciples plucked the ears of corn, and did eat, rubbing them in their hands.

2 And certain of the Pharisees said unto them, Why do ye that which is not lawful to do on the sabbath days?

3 And Jesus answering them said, Have ye not read so much as this, what David did, when himself was an hungred, and they which were with him;

4 How he went into the house of God, and did take and eat the shewbread, and gave also to them that were with him; which it is not lawful to eat but for the priests alone?

5 And he said unto them, That the Son of man is Lord also of the sabbath.

6 And it came to pass also on another sabbath, that he entered into the synagogue and taught: and there was a man whose right hand was withered.

7 And the scribes and Pharisees watched him, whether he would heal on the sabbath day; that they might find an accusation against him.

8 But he knew their thoughts, and said to the man which had the withered hand, Rise up, and stand forth in the midst. And he arose and stood forth.

9 Then said Jesus unto them, I will ask you one thing; Is it lawful on the sabbath days to do good, or to do evil? to save life, or to destroy it?

10 And looking round about upon them all, he said unto the man, Stretch forth thy hand. And he did so: and his hand was restored whole as the other.

11 And they were filled with madness; and communed one with another what they might do to Jesus.

A Sabbath-Day Healing

It is hard for the modern mind to understand the problem these verses present. According to the law, the disciples had a perfect right to gather the grain and eat it (Deuteronomy 23:25). The Pharisees are not objecting to their taking the grain. The problem is the act of rubbing the kernels. They interpret this as work, which is unlawful on the Sabbath.

1. Read Exodus 20:1–8. What is the fourth commandment?

A closer look, however, reveals that the Pharisees are the ones breaking the law, not the Lord's disciples. This incident probably occurred during the festival of Unleavened Bread (Luke 6:1). The disciples are eating grain directly from the stalks—it is certainly unleavened. This is not the problem. In the spiritual realm, however, hypocrisy is leaven (12:1). The Pharisees were guilty of hypocrisy and so were unlawfully adding leaven to the festival of Unleavened Bread.

Jesus Christ exposed them as hypocrites in this way: The priests of Israel labor in the temple on the Sabbath. Also, David ate the holy bread reserved for priests (1 Samuel 21:1–6). Why can't the disciples satisfy their hunger on the Sabbath? But more importantly, he himself is the Lord of the Sabbath. If he is not offended, why should the Pharisees be?

2. In Numbers 28:9–10, what work did the priests perform on the Sabbath?

The Lord frequently healed on the Sabbath. Here's why:

Christ's Sabbath-day healings were signs that pointed to the final healing of Israel. When the nation is cured of unbelief (Romans 11:26), it will enter into the great Sabbath of the thousand-year kingdom (Revelation 20:4). Today, this is commonly called the millennium. So, despite Israel's vain efforts to keep the Sabbath, "A Sabbath rest still remains for the people of God" (Hebrews 4:9 NRSV).

3. Hebrews 4:1 says "the promise of entering into his rest is still open" (NRSV). According to verse 3, how does one enter into that rest?

DAY FORTY-EIGHT

Luke 7:36–48

36 And one of the Pharisees desired him that he would eat with him. And he went into the Pharisee's house, and sat down to meat.

37 And, behold, a woman in the city, which was a sinner, when she knew that Jesus sat at meat in the Pharisee's house, brought an alabaster box of ointment,

38 And stood at his feet behind him weeping, and began to wash his feet with tears, and did wipe them with the hairs of her head, and kissed his feet, and anointed them with the ointment.

39 Now when the Pharisee which had bidden him saw it, he spake within himself, saying, This man, if he were a prophet, would have known who and what manner of woman this is that toucheth him: for she is a sinner.

40 And Jesus answering said unto him, Simon, I have somewhat to say unto thee. And he saith, Master, say on.

41 There was a certain creditor which had two debtors: the one owed five hundred pence, and the other fifty.

42 And when they had nothing to pay, he frankly forgave them both. Tell me therefore, which of them will love him most?

43 Simon answered and said, I suppose that he, to whom he forgave most. And he said unto him, Thou hast rightly judged.

44 And he turned to the woman, and said unto Simon, Seest thou this woman? I entered into thine house, thou gavest me no water for my feet: but she hath washed my feet with tears, and wiped them with the hairs of her head. . . .

47 Wherefore I say unto thee, Her sins, which are many, are forgiven; for she loved much: but to whom little is forgiven, the same loveth little.

48 And he said unto her, Thy sins are forgiven.

The Philosophy of Sin

Here are a Pharisee and a woman. One is at the top and the other at the bottom of the social scale. Since truth is best conveyed by contrast, note their different reactions to the grace of Christ.

Jesus loved sinners, yet his holiness remained pure. Simon, the self-righteous Pharisee, probably shudders to see this sinful woman touch the Lord. But it draws out compassion in Christ. Simon thinks his guest is unaware of her character. But the ignorance is not the Lord's or the woman's. Her tears, her worship, and all she does, show deep understanding of her sinfulness and his salvation.

Typical of all the leadership in Israel at that time, Simon the Pharisee is the ignorant one. He does not know his own sinfulness or recognize his Savior. He does not even honor him with the common courtesies of hospitality. If he knew the Lord, he would lavish attention on him and rejoice in the woman's worship.

1. Zechariah 12:10 describes Israel's reaction when Christ returns. What will they do then that the sinful woman does here?

This simple parable explains the philosophy of sin. That is, though hateful in itself, sin's ultimate effect is to produce an abundant response to God's love. The greatest triumphs of grace are in the darkest depths of degradation. This is clearly seen in the example of the apostle Paul who was "a blasphemer, a persecutor, and a man of violence"—the worst of sinners. But he testified, "The grace of our Lord was poured out on me abundantly, along with the faith and love that are in Christ Jesus" (1 Timothy 1:13–14, 16 NIV).

2. In 1 Corinthians 15:9, why was Paul unfit to be called an apostle? (See Acts 26:9–11.) What caused him to be fit for his apostleship?

The Pharisee supposes he is vastly superior to the outcast woman. But his love for the Savior is shallow and his response to grace feeble because he has no true sense of sin. We do not encourage or approve of sin. Still, we must accept its place in God's purpose to establish strong, warm relations with humanity. This cannot occur by any other means. As surprising as it may seem, this parable teaches that the more certain we are of the seriousness of our sin, the more certain will be our love for the one who died for sinners. This is the only revealed and rational explanation of the temporary presence of sin in the world.

3. According to Romans 5:20, what happens when sin increases?

Day Forty-Nine

Luke 8:22–25

22 Now it came to pass on a certain day, that he went into a ship with his disciples: and he said unto them, Let us go over unto the other side of the lake. And they launched forth.

23 But as they sailed he fell asleep: and there came down a storm of wind on the lake; and they were filled with water, and were in jeopardy.

24 And they came to him, and awoke him, saying, Master, master, we perish. Then he arose, and rebuked the wind and the raging of the water: and they ceased, and there was a calm.

25 And he said unto them, Where is your faith? And they being afraid wondered, saying one to another, What manner of man is this! for he commandeth even the winds and water, and they obey him.

The Storm of Crucifixion; The Calm of Resurrection

This story foretells the great spiritual storm that overwhelmed the disciples at the time of the Crucifixion. The wind represents the unseen powers of evil that swirled around them that day. One of these entered into Judas (Luke 22:3). The waters of the sea stand for the people who were whipped into fury by these evil powers.

1. Revelation 17:1 shows a woman who is seated on many waters. In verse 15, what do these waters represent?

On another occasion, the Lord was not present in the boat (John 6:16–21). That storm refers to the time of great tribulation at the end of this age (Matthew 24:21). Then, the Lord will come to his beloved people, walking on the turbulent waters. He will still the wind and the waves and bring Israel safely to land—the promised kingdom. He will bind Satan (Revelation 20:2), judge the nations (Matthew 25:31–46), and establish the kingdom (Revelation 11:15). Then will his words truly be fulfilled: "It is I; do not be afraid" (John 6:20 NRSV).

2. In John 6:16, at what time of day does the storm come upon the disciples?

During the storm in Luke's account, Christ is with them in the boat. But he falls asleep, indicating his death on the cross. This causes great fear in the apostles (Mark 14:50; John 20:19). The danger to the disciples is seen in the fact that their boat begins to swamp (Luke 8:23). Yet, the Lord awakens just as he will rise from the dead in resurrection. Then they will know Christ to be sovereign over all the powers of evil, not only wind and wave. But now they wonder what kind of man he is (v. 25). Death and resurrection will reveal this wonder to them.

3. In John 20:27, Jesus comes to the fearful disciples in resurrection. What does he say to them?

DAY FIFTY

Luke 9:43–56

43 And they were all amazed at the mighty power of God. But while they wondered every one at all things which Jesus did, he said unto his disciples,

44 Let these sayings sink down into your ears: for the Son of man shall be delivered into the hands of men.

45 But they understood not this saying, and it was hid from them, that they perceived it not: and they feared to ask him of that saying.

46 Then there arose a reasoning among them, which of them should be greatest.

47 And Jesus, perceiving the thought of their heart, took a child, and set him by him,

48 And said unto them, Whosoever shall receive this child in my name receiveth me: and whosoever shall receive me receiveth him that sent me: for he that is least among you all, the same shall be great.

49 And John answered and said, Master, we saw one casting out devils in thy name; and we forbad him, because he followeth not with us.

50 And Jesus said unto him, Forbid him not: for he that is not against us is for us.

51 And it came to pass, when the time was come that he should be received up, he stedfastly set his face to go to Jerusalem,

52 And sent messengers before his face: and they went, and entered into a village of the Samaritans, to make ready for him.

53 And they did not receive him, because his face was as though he would go to Jerusalem.

54 And when his disciples James and John saw this, they said, Lord, wilt thou that we command fire to come down from heaven, and consume them, even as Elias did?

55 But he turned, and rebuked them, and said, Ye know not what manner of spirit ye are of.

56 For the Son of man is not come to destroy men's lives, but to save them. And they went to another village.

The Distracted Disciples

Jesus Christ is determined to travel to Jerusalem to meet the moment of his greatest humiliation (Luke 9:51). What are the disciples thinking of at this time?

• They are concerned with their own exaltation (v. 46).

• They are in competition with other ministries (v. 49).

• They are judgmental toward those who oppose them (v. 54).

All this is occurring after Peter's revelation of the Messiah (v. 20); after Christ's transformation on the mountain (vv. 28–36); and after the healing of a demoniac child (vv. 37–43). Meanwhile, Christ ignores the amazement of the multitude over the child's healing (v. 44); their fickleness and unbelief are nothing new to him.

1. Read John 2:23–25. What is the Lord's response to the crowd that believes in him because of his miracles?

Concerned that the disciples will not be deceived by the sensational response to his miracle, the Lord urges the disciples, "Let these words sink into your ears" (Luke 9:44 NRSV). Peter, James, and John have just witnessed the marvelous manifestation on the mountain. They would naturally conclude that this is the time for the kingdom to come. So, the Lord contrasts the crowd's amazement with bitter words about his betrayal (v. 44). He wants the disciples to learn what is in man and to put no confidence in the flesh.

The Master reminds them, in plain speech, that he is to suffer and die. Still, they are ambitious, competitive, and judgmental. In a certain way, this is a more miserable manifestation of human perversity than the unbelief of the crowd.

2. Matthew 16:21 is the first plainspoken statement of the Lord's betrayal, death, and resurrection. What is Peter's response to this (v. 22)?

3. The disciples are thinking only of themselves in Luke 9:43–56. Compare Romans 8:7 with Matthew 16:23. What is the mind that is set on the flesh?

DAY FIFTY-ONE

Luke 10:25–37

25 And, behold, a certain lawyer stood up, and tempted him, saying, Master, what shall I do to inherit eternal life?

26 He said unto him, What is written in the law? how readest thou?

27 And he answering said, Thou shalt love the Lord thy God with all thy heart, and with all thy soul, and with all thy strength, and with all thy mind; and thy neighbour as thyself.

28 And he said unto him, Thou hast answered right: this do, and thou shalt live.

29 But he, willing to justify himself, said unto Jesus, And who is my neighbour?

30 And Jesus answering said, A certain man went down from Jerusalem to Jericho, and fell among thieves, which stripped him of his raiment, and wounded him, and departed, leaving him half dead.

31 And by chance there came down a certain priest that way: and when he saw him, he passed by on the other side.

32 And likewise a Levite, when he was at the place, came and looked on him, and passed by on the other side.

33 But a certain Samaritan, as he journeyed, came where he was: and when he saw him, he had compassion on him,

34 And went to him, and bound up his wounds, pouring in oil and wine, and set him on his own beast, and brought him to an inn, and took care of him.

35 And on the morrow when he departed, he took out two pence, and gave them to the host, and said unto him, Take care of him; and whatsoever thou spendest more, when I come again, I will repay thee.

36 Which now of these three, thinkest thou, was neighbour unto him that fell among the thieves?

37 And he said, He that shewed mercy on him. Then said Jesus unto him, Go, and do thou likewise.

Christ the Samaritan

Here is how the Lord described the religious lawyers of his day: "You load people with burdens hard to bear, and you yourselves do not lift a finger to ease them" (Luke 11:46 NRSV). Naturally, such a person would be interested in the Lord's opinion as to what deeds merit eternal life. According to Moses' law, this is simple: "You shall keep my statues and my ordinances; by doing so, one shall live" (Leviticus 18:5 NRSV).

The Lord questions him: "What is written in the law? (Luke 10:56). In reply, the lawyer narrates the greatest commandment—love to God (Deuteronomy 6:5), and its complement—love to man (Leviticus 19:18). This reveals that he knows the law quite well, so the Lord points out that all he needs to do is keep the law. If he could do this, he would never die. But the law was not given to impart life. It was given to cause death.

1. Read Romans 3:20. What does one learn by keeping the law?

Like a true lawyer, this man quibbles over terminology: "Who is my neighbor?"

This brings us to the parable of the Good Samaritan. Jesus Christ tells this story to show the uselessness of laws and ceremonies and, more importantly, to reveal himself as the Savior of Israel's law keepers. The Jews despised the Samaritans (John 4:9). The lawyer would never accept one as his neighbor. The Lord was also despised and so enters the story as the hated Samaritan.

2. Read 2 Kings 17:24–28. Who replaced the Israelites in the cities of Samaria?

The lawyer is like the man in the parable who is descending from Jerusalem to Jericho. Jerusalem is the place of blessing and life. These are his possession if he keeps the law. Jericho is the place of the curse, which is his if he breaks the law (Joshua 6:26). He has left the blessing and is on his way to the curse because, despite his scriptural knowledge, he cannot keep the law.

3. Compare Deuteronomy 27:26 and Galatians 3:10. What becomes of people who do not keep the law?

The law brings death, so the man is half dead on the road. Will religious rites help him? This hope is dashed when a priest comes along and keeps as far from him as he can. It is not that he is hardhearted. According to the law, a priest cannot defile himself with the dead. The Levite also cannot be defiled with the dead. In other words, the law cannot help a man in his condition. It does not cure, but condemns. The priest and Levite possess religious holiness but are helpless to love their neighbor as the law demands.

The priest and Levite happen along by chance (Luke 10:31–32). But the Samaritan is on a journey (v. 33). Like the Lord, he is on a definite mission of salvation. The wounded man does not repel but rather attracts and draws out the Samaritan's compassion. The Samaritan is not defiled by contact with death or sin. The half-dead Jew by the roadside, under other circumstances, would no doubt hate the Samaritan. But the despicable Samaritan rescues him and displays love not only for his neighbor, but also for his enemy. He rises far above the law's demands.

4. Jesus Christ not only fulfilled the law, he uplifted it. Read Matthew 5:43–45. How did the Lord uplift the law of Leviticus 19:18?

DAY FIFTY-TWO

Luke 11:14–23

14 And he was casting out a devil, and it was dumb. And it came to pass, when the devil was gone out, the dumb spake; and the people wondered.

15 But some of them said, He casteth out devils through Beelzebub the chief of the devils.

16 And others, tempting him, sought of him a sign from heaven.

17 But he, knowing their thoughts, said unto them, Every kingdom divided against itself is brought to desolation; and a house divided against a house falleth.

18 If Satan also be divided against himself, how shall his kingdom stand? because ye say that I cast out devils through Beelzebub.

19 And if I by Beelzebub cast out devils, by whom do your sons cast them out? therefore shall they be your judges.

20 But if I with the finger of God cast out devils, no doubt the kingdom of God is come upon you.

21 When a strong man armed keepeth his palace, his goods are in peace:

22 But when a stronger than he shall come upon him, and overcome him, he taketh from him all his armour wherein he trusted, and divideth his spoils.

23 He that is not with me is against me: and he that gathereth not with me scattereth.

Christ's Spiritual Warfare

As John the Baptist and Jesus preached the nearness of the kingdom of the heavens (Matthew 3:2; 4:17), demonic activity increased. This is why there are so many cases of casting out demons in the Gospels (Acts 2:22). These signs display the Lord's impressive spiritual power. The demons are emissaries and subordinates of Satan (Mark 11:18). Every one of them forced to leave its victim is a sign pointing to the ejection of Satan himself at the beginning of the kingdom.

1. Compare Exodus 8:19 with Luke 11:20. What did the Lord use to cast out demons?

2. According to Revelation 20:1–3, for how long is Satan bound?

The most important factor in the millennial kingdom is the absence of Satan. From Adam's temptation in Eden to the end of this age, man's hostility to God is the result of external, wicked spiritual influences (Ephesians 6:12). Humanity is the pawn that is played by Satan in his efforts to overthrow God's sovereignty (1 Peter 5:8). The release of mankind from this control is essential to the establishment of righteous government. Men's efforts fail chiefly because they do not account for this influence. It is unknown to them. Even if they were aware of its presence, they would not be able to cope with it (Ephesians 4:17–18).

3. According to 1 John 5:9, who controls the world?

Every time the Lord or his disciples cast out a demon, the kingdom is previewed. Satan's influence over mankind will culminate when he is cast down to earth (Revelation 12:3, 7–9). As the seven-headed dragon (v. 3), he personally assumes the leadership of man's campaign against God at the time of the end. Then Christ will descend and cut his career short by confining him for the thousand years (19:11–16; 20:3).

Day Fifty-Three

Luke 12:41–48

41 Then Peter said unto him, Lord, speakest thou this parable unto us, or even to all?

42 And the Lord said, Who then is that faithful and wise steward, whom his lord shall make ruler over his household, to give them their portion of meat in due season?

43 Blessed is that servant, whom his lord when he cometh shall find so doing.

44 Of a truth I say unto you, that he will make him ruler over all that he hath.

45 But and if that servant say in his heart, My lord delayeth his coming; and shall begin to beat the menservants and maidens, and to eat and drink, and to be drunken;

46 The lord of that servant will come in a day when he looketh not for him, and at an hour when he is not aware, and will cut him in sunder, and will appoint him his portion with the unbelievers.

47 And that servant, which knew his lord's will, and prepared not himself, neither did according to his will, shall be beaten with many stripes.

48 But he that knew not, and did commit things worthy of stripes, shall be beaten with few stripes. For unto whomsoever much is given, of him shall be much required: and to whom men have committed much, of him they will ask the more.

Coming as a Thief; Coming as a Savior

The coming of Christ as the Son of Man will be a complete surprise even to those who are watching for him (Luke 12:46). He will come to Israel like a thief in the night with sudden destruction for those in darkness (Matthew 24:42–44; 1 Thessalonians 5:2–3). But we who today are believers in Christ are not in darkness. So, that day will not overtake us like a thief (vv. 4–5). God has not destined us for wrath, but for salvation through our Lord Jesus Christ (v. 9).

1. According to Philippians 3:20, what are we expecting
   Christ to be when he comes for us?

Matthew 24 is mainly concerned with Israel at the end of this age
(v. 3). Verses 43 and 44 say that those in Israel who at that time are expecting the Lord's coming must stay awake and be ready. Luke 12:46–47
indicates the same thing. The Lord's coming for us, on the other hand, is
a matter of pure grace. Certainly, we should joyfully anticipate it, but even
if we are distracted from it, this will not cost us our place in his presence.
Our salvation depends on his death, not our faithfulness (Ephesians 1:7).

2. Ephesians 2:8 explains what saves us and what does not.
   What are these two things?

This parable shows that some in Israel will be rewarded for service
at his coming others will be punished for unfaithfulness. They are
dealt with like servants. Their place in the kingdom depends on their
works during their Lord's absence. But we are subjects of grace and,
though we may suffer loss for unfaithfulness, we ourselves will be
saved (1 Corinthians 3:15).

3. 1 Thessalonians 4:16–18 tells of his coming for the
   church. What effect should these words have upon us?
   (See verse 18.)

Day Fifty-Four

Luke 13:22–30

22 And he went through the cities and villages, teaching, and journeying toward Jerusalem.

23 Then said one unto him, Lord, are there few that be saved? And he said unto them,

24 Strive to enter in at the strait gate: for many, I say unto you, will seek to enter in, and shall not be able.

25 When once the master of the house is risen up, and hath shut to the door, and ye begin to stand without, and to knock at the door, saying, Lord, Lord, open unto us; and he shall answer and say unto you, I know you not whence ye are:

26 Then shall ye begin to say, We have eaten and drunk in thy presence, and thou hast taught in our streets.

27 But he shall say, I tell you, I know you not whence ye are; depart from me, all ye workers of iniquity.

28 There shall be weeping and gnashing of teeth, when ye shall see Abraham, and Isaac, and Jacob, and all the prophets, in the kingdom of God, and you yourselves thrust out.

29 And they shall come from the east, and from the west, and from the north, and from the south, and shall sit down in the kingdom of God.

30 And, behold, there are last which shall be first, and there are first which shall be last.

The Gate of the Gospel

Someone asks, "Lord, will only a few be saved?" (Luke 13:23). Up to this time, the gates of the kingdom were open wide; all Israel could be saved. It was easy to enter by repentance and baptism. But this entrance has closed (Matthew 13:13–15), as illustrated by the following facts:

• Jesus Christ has informed his followers of his betrayal, death, and resurrection (9:22).

- He is determined to go to his appointment at the cross in Jerusalem (9:51; 13:22).

- The religious leaders of Israel have accused the Lord of being in league with Satan (Luke 11:15), rejecting his godly commission as their Messiah.

  1. In Luke 11:52, what did the Pharisees do to others in Israel who wanted to enter the kingdom? (See also Matthew 23:13.)

Like the gate into the courtyard of a rich man's house, the gate into the kingdom is wide. It is not hard to enter. But, because of Israel's hardness, this gate has closed (v. 25). Such a house also had narrow side doors that were closed at night. Not long after the Lord's resurrection and ascension, the gate to the kingdom is again thrown wide open through Peter's preaching.

  2. Read Acts 2:36. To whom is Peter preaching?

  3. In Acts 2:38, what did Israel have to do to enter the kingdom?

The parable in Luke 13:24–30 should not be applied to today's gospel of the grace of God. Our Good News is not narrow or cramped. It is even wider than Israel's kingdom gospel. It includes all nations unconditionally. Faith is not a narrow door through which one must struggle. God is not reluctant to save mankind. God is conciliated and pleads everyone to be reconciled with him (2 Corinthians 5:20).

  4. In 2 Corinthians 5:19, what is God's attitude toward the sins of mankind?

Day Fifty-Five

Luke 15:1–10

1 Then drew near unto him all the publicans and sinners for to hear him.

2 And the Pharisees and scribes murmured, saying, This man receiveth sinners, and eateth with them.

3 And he spake this parable unto them, saying,

4 What man of you, having an hundred sheep, if he lose one of them, doth not leave the ninety and nine in the wilderness, and go after that which is lost, until he find it?

5 And when he hath found it, he layeth it on his shoulders, rejoicing.

6 And when he cometh home, he calleth together his friends and neighbours, saying unto them, Rejoice with me; for I have found my sheep which was lost.

7 I say unto you, that likewise joy shall be in heaven over one sinner that repenteth, more than over ninety and nine just persons, which need no repentance.

8 Either what woman having ten pieces of silver, if she lose one piece, doth not light a candle, and sweep the house, and seek diligently till she find it?

9 And when she hath found it, she calleth her friends and her neighbours together, saying, Rejoice with me; for I have found the piece which I had lost.

10 Likewise, I say unto you, there is joy in the presence of the angels of God over one sinner that repenteth.

The Five-Fold Parable—The Lost Sheep and the Lost Coin

The Lord loves sinners. So, the self-righteous Pharisees and scribes unintentionally speak a precious truth: "This man is receiving sinners!" (Luke 15:2 NRSV). Christ makes their accusation the basis of a five-fold parable (v. 3). In this, he emphasizes that God is not concerned with the self-righteous but with those who realize they are sinners. The parable includes the stories of the lost sheep, the lost coin, the two sons, the unjust manager, and the rich man and Lazarus. These are five different parts of one parable that deals with the classes of people in the nation of Israel at that time. Like all the parables, these are not simply examples of divine truth, but illustrations of spiritual facts concerning Israel at that time. First, the story of the lost sheep tells of the Savior's attitude toward those who are lost.

1. According to Matthew 15:24, to whom was the Lord sent? (See also Acts 3:25–26.)

Christ never left the land of Israel to reach other nations. His commission was to Israel. Through them, God will bless all the nations of the world (Genesis 22:18). The one hundred sheep represent the nation of Israel. The Lord is their good shepherd (John 10:11). The ninety-nine sheep are the self-righteous majority of Israel, like the Pharisees and scribes to whom Christ is speaking. These think they do not need to repent. This attitude leaves them out in the wilderness, far from the shelter of the fold, without the shepherd's protection, and open to the attacks of wild beasts. These attacks will come in full force during the great tribulation at the end of this age (Matthew 24:21).

2. Read John 10:11. What does the good shepherd do for the sheep?

Self-righteous people think they are safe. They don't call out for God's help. The one crying sheep that strays from the flock causes the Lord more suffering and gives him more joy than all the rest (Luke 15:6). God was not satisfied with Israel because of their self-righteousness. In contrast, the straying tax gatherers and sinners heard the Son's voice gladly (John 10:4). Only they responded to his love and mercy. He received sinners because the others would not have him. They didn't even feel the need for a savior.

The hunt for a lost sheep in the wilds of Judea was a dangerous task. This is a reminder of the Lord's suffering and death on the cross, which was like descending into a deep dark ravine infested with savage beasts.

3. Read Isaiah 53:6. What has the Lord done for the straying sheep?

The story of the lost sheep shows God's side of the story. Since the nation is often depicted as a woman, the story of the lost coin tells of Israel's point of view. Traditionally, women of the land wear silver coins for ornaments as in a headdress. These are most prized, and mean much more than their cash value.

4. In Isaiah 61:10, what are the garments of salvation?

In love, God had decked Israel with ornaments (Ezekiel 16:11–13). In this story, one of these ornaments is missing; its loss means that the nation has lost its beauty (v. 15).

The Pharisees accuse Christ of welcoming sinners. Little do they know that each lost sinner they witness turning back to God is a preview of the day when all Israel will be saved and again be dressed in the garments of salvation (Romans 11:26).

Day Fifty-Six

Luke 15:11–32

11 And he said, A certain man had two sons:

12 And the younger of them said to his father, Father, give me the portion of goods that falleth to me. And he divided unto them his living.

13 And not many days after the younger son gathered all together, and took his journey into a far country, and there wasted his substance with riotous living.

14 And when he had spent all, there arose a mighty famine in that land; and he began to be in want.

15 And he went and joined himself to a citizen of that country; and he sent him into his fields to feed swine.

16 And he would fain have filled his belly with the husks that the swine did eat: and no man gave unto him.

17 And when he came to himself, he said, How many hired servants of my father's have bread enough and to spare, and I perish with hunger!

18 I will arise and go to my father, and will say unto him, Father, I have sinned against heaven, and before thee,

19 And am no more worthy to be called thy son: make me as one of thy hired servants.

20 And he arose, and came to his father. But when he was yet a great way off, his father saw him, and had compassion, and ran, and fell on his neck, and kissed him.

21 And the son said unto him, Father, I have sinned against heaven, and in thy sight, and am no more worthy to be called thy son.

22 But the father said to his servants, Bring forth the best robe, and put it on him; and put a ring on his hand, and shoes on his feet:

23 And bring hither the fatted calf, and kill it; and let us eat, and be merry:

24 For this my son was dead, and is alive again; he was lost, and is found. And they began to be merry.

25 Now his elder son was in the field: and as he came and drew nigh to the house, he heard musick and dancing.

26 And he called one of the servants, and asked what these things meant.

27 And he said unto him, Thy brother is come; and thy father hath killed the fatted calf, because he hath received him safe and sound.

28 And he was angry, and would not go in: therefore came his father out, and intreated him.

29 And he answering said to his father, Lo, these many years do I serve thee, neither transgressed I at any time thy commandment: and yet thou never gavest me a kid, that I might make merry with my friends:

30 But as soon as this thy son was come, which hath devoured thy living with harlots, thou hast killed for him the fatted calf.

31 And he said unto him, Son, thou art ever with me, and all that I have is thine.

32 It was meet that we should make merry, and be glad: for this thy brother was dead, and is alive again; and was lost, and is found.

The Five-Fold Parable—The Two Sons

The parable of the two sons paints a portrait of the two classes in Israel that shows their moral distance from God. The prodigal son is far from the father's house; the elder son is far from his father's heart. The Pharisees and scribes boast of their nearness to God. They are always in the temple, but their hearts are far from God. The tax collectors and sinners are outcasts from the Jewish nation and religion. They have no place in the temple, yet they know their predicament and crave the loving mercy of God.

1. Read Isaiah 29:13. How does this verse describe the worship of people whose hearts are far from God?

Religion like that of the self-righteous Pharisees and scribes is based on conduct. The elder son illustrates their right living and lawkeeping. But such behavior, even if sincere and true, does not allow the Father a chance to reveal his affection. The debauchery and decadence of the prodigal son are like those of the sinners. He joins the citizens of a foreign country, keeps hogs, and even desires the diet of those unclean creatures. This is just like the traitorous tax collectors who joined with Rome in oppressing Israel.

2. In Jeremiah 31:18–20, the tribe of Ephraim represents Israel. In verse 20, what does the Lord call Ephraim? How does God feel about Ephraim? What will God do for Ephraim?

Like the prodigal son, a person who is far from God often does not understand the Father's love. The prodigal intends to plead for a place in his father's service (Luke 15:19). He rehearses a little speech. His highest expectation is to be a servant, not a son. But his father ignores all this and gives him the highest place of honor in his house. The best robe covers his filthiness; sandals protect his feet; a ring beautifies the hand that had fed the swine. The father delights in his son's return. Feasting and merriment begin and have no end (v. 24).

It is the same with the outcasts of Israel: The Lord freely forgives them. They are not put on probation; they do not have to make amends through good conduct. They simply sit down and feast with Jesus Christ, enjoying the grace of God. The elder brother has no such enjoyment, though he has spent his whole life in his father's house keeping the commandments (Luke 15:29). In fact, he complains about his father's joyful celebration, just as the Pharisees always object to Christ's consorting with sinners.

3. In Job 33:27–28, someone sings, "I sinned, and perverted what was right" (NRSV). What is God's response to this?

One day, Israel will sit down in the kingdom at the wedding supper of the Lamb (Revelation 19:9). In the consummation, all creation will rejoice when God is all in all (1 Corinthians 15:24, 28). These triumphs do not have their source in the elder son's obedience, but in the prodigal son's disgrace and defiance. Sin's destruction and death reveal God's unconditional love: "This son of mine was dead and is alive again; he was lost and is found" (Luke 15:24 NRSV).

4. In Romans 5:21, why does sin reign in death?

Day Fifty-Seven

Luke 16:1–13

1 And he said also unto his disciples, There was a certain rich man, which had a steward; and the same was accused unto him that he had wasted his goods.

2 And he called him, and said unto him, How is it that I hear this of thee? give an account of thy stewardship; for thou mayest be no longer steward.

3 Then the steward said within himself, What shall I do? for my lord taketh away from me the stewardship: I cannot dig; to beg I am ashamed.

4 I am resolved what to do, that, when I am put out of the stewardship, they may receive me into their houses.

5 So he called every one of his lord's debtors unto him, and said unto the first, How much owest thou unto my lord?

6 And he said, An hundred measures of oil. And he said unto him, Take thy bill, and sit down quickly, and write fifty. . . .

8 And the lord commended the unjust steward, because he had done wisely: for the children of this world are in their generation wiser than the children of light.

9 And I say unto you, Make to yourselves friends of the mammon of unrighteousness; that, when ye fail, they may receive you into everlasting habitations.

10 He that is faithful in that which is least is faithful also in much: and he that is unjust in the least is unjust also in much.

11 If therefore ye have not been faithful in the unrighteous mammon, who will commit to your trust the true riches? . . .

13 No servant can serve two masters: for either he will hate the one, and love the other; or else he will hold to the one, and despise the other. Ye cannot serve God and mammon.

The Five-Fold Parable—The Unjust Manager

The parable of the unjust manager exposes the motives of the Pharisees and scribes. They were the stewards of Israel's spiritual wealth. But they dissipated those treasures, were fond of money, and served their own greed rather than ministering for God's glory. They were so shrewd in the things of this life that they jeopardized their prospects in the ages to come.

1. 1 Timothy 6:17 advises that we set our hopes on God rather than uncertain riches. According to verse 19, what is the benefit of heeding this advice?

The unjust manager was exceptionally shrewd, so his master praised him (Luke 16:8). Judging by appearances, this child of the world was wiser than any child of light.

2. In Ephesians 5:8–9, where can one find the fruit of light?

The manager's master gives him this advice: "And I tell you, make friends for yourselves by means of dishonest wealth so that when it is gone, they may welcome you into the eternal homes" (v. 9 NRSV). Note that this statement is not in the voice of Christ. The Lord does not admire unrighteousness or advise deceit. In fact, the following verse is opposed to such double-dealing. There, Christ tells his listeners that faithfulness, not shrewdness, will bring honor in the kingdom (v. 10).

Verse 9 indicates that the Pharisees used their riches to maintain their positions of influence, their "friends" so to speak, in Israel. They loved the praise of men more than the praise of God (John 12:43 NIV). Nonetheless, they thought their privileges would carry over into the kingdom age. Though they died rich, the Pharisees will have no place in the glories of the Messianic reign. Christ died in poverty, yet he will be weighted with the wealth of earth's highest glories.

3. According to James 4:4, what happens when one becomes a friend of the world?

DAY FIFTY-EIGHT

Luke 16:19–31

19 There was a certain rich man, which was clothed in purple and fine linen, and fared sumptuously every day:

20 And there was a certain beggar named Lazarus, which was laid at his gate, full of sores,

21 And desiring to be fed with the crumbs which fell from the rich man's table: moreover the dogs came and licked his sores.

22 And it came to pass, that the beggar died, and was carried by the angels into Abraham's bosom: the rich man also died, and was buried;

23 And in hell he lift up his eyes, being in torments, and seeth Abraham afar off, and Lazarus in his bosom.

24 And he cried and said, Father Abraham, have mercy on me, and send Lazarus, that he may dip the tip of his finger in water, and cool my tongue; for I am tormented in this flame.

25 But Abraham said, Son, remember that thou in thy lifetime receivedst thy good things, and likewise Lazarus evil things: but now he is comforted, and thou art tormented.

26 And beside all this, between us and you there is a great gulf fixed: so that they which would pass from hence to you cannot; neither can they pass to us, that would come from thence.

27 Then he said, I pray thee therefore, father, that thou wouldest send him to my father's house:

28 For I have five brethren; that he may testify unto them, lest they also come into this place of torment.

29 Abraham saith unto him, They have Moses and the prophets; let them hear them.

30 And he said, Nay, father Abraham: but if one went unto them from the dead, they will repent.

31 And he said unto him, If they hear not Moses and the prophets, neither will they be persuaded, though one rose from the dead.

The Five-Fold Parable—Lazarus and the Rich Man

The story of the unjust manager explains that the Pharisees' stewardship of God's spiritual riches is to be terminated. A statement about divorce immediately follows this (Luke 16:18). Though apparently unconnected, this verse suggests that the entire nation is to be divorced from Jehovah. This is an appropriate link to lead us to the final section of the five-fold parable. The story of Lazarus and the rich man discusses Israel's fate during her divorce, before her reunion with God at Christ's return.

1. In Isaiah 54:5, what is the maker's relationship with Israel?

2. Revelation 19 tells of the return of Christ. In verse 7, how is Israel depicted?

The rich man is dressed in fine linen and purple. Linen is the garment of Israel's priests; purple is the color of kings. This indicates Israel as the royal priesthood (Exodus 19:6). His sumptuous feasting points to Israel's special blessings. The privileged Pharisees demeaned the sinners and tax collectors. Their place was outside with Lazarus and the dogs just as the prodigal son lived far off with the swine.

3. In Ezekiel 16:48–50, Israel is called the sister of Sodom. In verse 49, what is the guilt of Sodom?

The rich man in the flames shows the nation that has deserted God and God's truth. Lazarus on the other hand is comforted in Abraham's bosom. He represents Israel's faithful remnant. Both are dead in this story. So long as the nation is divorced from her divine husband, neither Lazarus nor the rich man can enjoy the blessings of the kingdom (Hebrews 11:13–16).

The flames in which the rich man suffers prophetically picture the persecution and hatred of the Jewish nation through history. The comfort that was found by those few who believed is seen in the figure of Abraham's bosom. The tax collectors and sinners who feasted with the Lord, who were the subject of the Pharisees' constant complaints, were in reality enjoying the bosom of Abraham. Everything in this scene is figurative. Abraham is not literally there, neither is Lazarus, the rich man, or the flames. Each represents something else.

The suffering rich man makes a remarkable request (Luke 16:28). He asks that Lazarus be resurrected and sent to warn his five brothers. Abraham replies that the brothers will not be convinced "even if someone rises from the dead" (v. 31). The Pharisees and scribes listening to this story correspond to the rich man's five brothers. After Jesus Christ is gone from the scene, they will hear Peter declare,

> *This man, handed over to you according to the definite plan and foreknowledge of God, you crucified and killed by the hands of those outside the law. But God raised him up, having freed him from death, because it was impossible for him to be held in its power (Acts 2:23–24 NIV).*

Some of these men may have perished forty years later in the horrific flames of the siege of Jerusalem (AD 70). Their descendants faced the ovens of the Holocaust. To this day, the Jews are besieged by national hatred. But the time of their restoration is drawing near (Romans 11:11–12). Before the rich man's torment ends, however, it will be intensified in the terror of the greatest of all Jewish persecutions (Matthew 24:21–22).

4. In Acts 1:8, the disciples are sent to their countrymen as witnesses of the resurrected Christ. Where are they to go and do this?

Day Fifty-Nine

Luke 17:20–37

20 And when he was demanded of the Pharisees, when the kingdom of God should come, he answered them and said, The kingdom of God cometh not with observation:

21 Neither shall they say, Lo here! or, lo there! for, behold, the kingdom of God is within you.

22 And he said unto the disciples, The days will come, when ye shall desire to see one of the days of the Son of man, and ye shall not see it.

23 And they shall say to you, See here; or, see there: go not after them, nor follow them.

24 For as the lightning, that lighteneth out of the one part under heaven, shineth unto the other part under heaven; so shall also the Son of man be in his day.

25 But first must he suffer many things, and be rejected of this generation.

26 And as it was in the days of Noe, so shall it be also in the days of the Son of man.

27 They did eat, they drank, they married wives, they were given in marriage, until the day that Noah entered into the ark, and the flood came, and destroyed them all.

28 Likewise also as it was in the days of Lot; they did eat, they drank, they bought, they sold, they planted, they builded;

29 But the same day that Lot went out of Sodom it rained fire and brimstone from heaven, and destroyed them all.

30 Even thus shall it be in the day when the Son of man is revealed.

31 In that day, he which shall be upon the housetop, and his stuff in the house, let him not come down to take it away: and he that is in the field, let him likewise not return back.

32 Remember Lot's wife.

33 Whosoever shall seek to save his life shall lose it; and whosoever shall lose his life shall preserve it.

34 I tell you, in that night there shall be two men in one bed; the one shall be taken, and the other shall be left.

35 Two women shall be grinding together; the one shall be taken, and the other left.

36 Two men shall be in the field; the one shall be taken, and the other left.

37 And they answered and said unto him, Where, Lord? And he said unto them, Wheresoever the body is, thither will the eagles be gathered together.

The Coming of the Kingdom

The scriptures clearly testify that the coming of the kingdom is a visible, observable event. It is like a lightning flash that instantly illuminates the entire earth (Luke 17:24). Signs and warnings in heaven as well as on earth go together with it. All see it.

1. According to Luke 21:25, where will signs occur before the kingdom comes?

The King James Version translates Luke 17:20 like this: "The kingdom of God cometh not with observation" This means that one cannot miss seeing the kingdom come. Careful scrutiny is unnecessary. Plus, the kingdom is not limited to any particular region but instantly covers the whole earth. It is useless to investigate or follow up any report that the kingdom is here or there (v. 23). When it comes, it will be everywhere.

2. Compare Luke 17:25 with 9:22. What is the first sign of the coming of the kingdom?

This does not deny the Lord's statement that "the kingdom of God is within you" (v. 21). All other kingdoms eventually fail because their citizens lack an inward response to its outward regulations and conditions. Christ's physical kingdom will be founded on a moral force within the human heart. Jesus Christ is here speaking with the Pharisees (v. 20). Like Nicodemus (John 3:1–3), they need an inward renewal to enter the kingdom.

3. How does John 3:6 fulfill one of the promises in Ezekiel 36:26?

The unexpected suddenness of the Lord's coming is seen in a comparison with the days of Noah (Luke 17:26). It will be a day of imagined security and swift destruction. Whereas the present day of grace has mercifully carried on for nearly two thousand years, the day of God's judgment is mercifully swift and sudden.

4. According to Matthew 24:38–39, what were the people in Noah's time doing just before the flood? (See Genesis 7.)

Day Sixty

Luke 18:31–43

31 Then he took unto him the twelve, and said unto them, Behold, we go up to Jerusalem, and all things that are written by the prophets concerning the Son of man shall be accomplished.

32 For he shall be delivered unto the Gentiles, and shall be mocked, and spitefully entreated, and spitted on:

33 And they shall scourge him, and put him to death: and the third day he shall rise again.

34 And they understood none of these things: and this saying was hid from them, neither knew they the things which were spoken.

35 And it came to pass, that as he was come nigh unto Jericho, a certain blind man sat by the way side begging:

36 And hearing the multitude pass by, he asked what it meant.

37 And they told him, that Jesus of Nazareth passeth by.

38 And he cried, saying, Jesus, thou son of David, have mercy on me.

39 And they which went before rebuked him, that he should hold his peace: but he cried so much the more, Thou son of David, have mercy on me.

40 And Jesus stood, and commanded him to be brought unto him: and when he was come near, he asked him,

41 Saying, What wilt thou that I shall do unto thee? And he said, Lord, that I may receive my sight.

42 And Jesus said unto him, Receive thy sight: thy faith hath saved thee.

43 And immediately he received his sight, and followed him, glorifying God: and all the people, when they saw it, gave praise unto God.

Blind to Christ

The Lord takes the twelve disciples aside for a brief conference. They still cannot understand the plainspoken predictions of his sufferings, even though he has repeated and emphasized them throughout this last journey to Jerusalem (Luke 18:34). Why is this? The disciples are preoccupied with the rewards they imagine are theirs in the future (Mark 10:35–37). This blinds them to the fact of their Master's great sacrifice, not to mention its meaning. No wonder Israel will ignorantly execute their Messiah. Even his closest associates cannot see that this will fulfill the predictions of the prophets that were read constantly in the synagogues (Luke 18:31).

1. What does Isaiah 53:10 predict God will do to the Messiah?

As in other accounts of the Lord's visit to Jericho, a man is healed of blindness immediately after the disciples' spiritual blindness is exposed. The healing of the blind is a sign that Christ will one day open the eyes of the blind nation. This happens partially when Christ is preached on the day of Pentecost (Acts 2–4). It comes in full at the end of this age when Israel sees the one whom they pierced, and the nation is born in a day (Zechariah 12:10; Isaiah 66:8).

The disciples precede Israel in the full revelation of Christ, his sufferings, and triumph. This begins after the Crucifixion on the road from Jerusalem to Emmaus (Luke 24:13–33). There, the resurrected Christ uses the scriptures to explain himself and his sufferings (vv. 25–27). Still today, when God's Spirit illuminates the scriptures our inner eyes are opened to see Christ in their pages.

2. Read Luke 24:19, what do the disciples call Jesus of Nazareth that shows they still do not know who he is? In verse 26, what does he call himself?

3. In Acts 2:31, Peter interprets Psalm 16:9–10. What is that interpretation?

DAY SIXTY-ONE

Luke 19:1–10

1 And Jesus entered and passed through Jericho.

2 And, behold, there was a man named Zacchaeus, which was the chief among the publicans, and he was rich.

3 And he sought to see Jesus who he was; and could not for the press, because he was little of stature.

4 And he ran before, and climbed up into a sycomore tree to see him: for he was to pass that way.

5 And when Jesus came to the place, he looked up, and saw him, and said unto him, Zacchaeus, make haste, and come down; for to day I must abide at thy house.

6 And he made haste, and came down, and received him joyfully.

7 And when they saw it, they all murmured, saying, That he was gone to be guest with a man that is a sinner.

8 And Zacchaeus stood, and said unto the Lord: Behold, Lord, the half of my goods I give to the poor; and if I have taken any thing from any man by false accusation, I restore him fourfold.

9 And Jesus said unto him, This day is salvation come to this house, forsomuch as he also is a son of Abraham.

10 For the Son of man is come to seek and to save that which was lost.

Despicable Zacchaeus

Zacchaeus was one of Israel's leading tax collectors—the most hated and unpopular people in the entire nation. They paid Rome the taxes for a particular district and then collected the tax from the people and enriched themselves by adding their own charges to it.

The Lord, the promised Messiah of Israel's independent kingdom, has one of these hated men among his apostles—Matthew (Matthew 9:9). How strange this must seem to the onlookers. Now, he invites himself to the house of a chief of these unpatriotic traitors. Nothing can more clearly show that Christ came to call sinners, not the righteous (Luke 5:32). This is a difficult lesson to learn. How better to teach it than through despicable Zacchaeus?

Zacchaeus's physical state corresponds to his spiritual condition. His small stature suggests his low esteem among his countrymen. But he elevates himself above them by climbing a sycamore tree. This tree was actually a fig-mulberry, or wild fig tree. The scriptures often use the cultivated fig tree to represent political Israel. The wild fig is an apt image of the Roman rule in Israel that gave Zacchaeus his position and wealth.

The Lord does not want him to remain in that position. "Hurry!" he says to the little man, "Come down" (Luke 19:5), and is welcomed into Zacchaeus's house. The effect of this is striking. Without any prompting, the tax collector announces his intention to give half of his possessions to the poor and to right his wrongdoings (v. 8).

1. Zacchaeus is one of the few people in Israel at that time who acted on John the Baptist's advice in Luke 3:8. What is that advice?

2. Zacchaeus has something in common with the sinful woman in Luke 7:36–50. What is this? (See verse 47.)

3. In Luke 19:9 Jesus calls Zacchaeus a child of Abraham. According to Galatians 3:6–7, what makes him a child of Abraham?

DAY SIXTY-TWO

Luke 20:9–19

9 Then began he to speak to the people this parable; A certain man planted a vineyard, and let it forth to husbandmen, and went into a far country for a long time.

10 And at the season he sent a servant to the husbandmen, that they should give him of the fruit of the vineyard: but the husbandmen beat him, and sent him away empty.

11 And again he sent another servant: and they beat him also, and entreated him shamefully, and sent him away empty.

12 And again he sent a third: and they wounded him also, and cast him out.

13 Then said the lord of the vineyard, What shall I do? I will send my beloved son: it may be they will reverence him when they see him.

14 But when the husbandmen saw him, they reasoned among themselves, saying, This is the heir: come, let us kill him, that the inheritance may be ours.

15 So they cast him out of the vineyard, and killed him. What therefore shall the lord of the vineyard do unto them?

16 He shall come and destroy these husbandmen, and shall give the vineyard to others. And when they heard it, they said, God forbid.

17 And he beheld them, and said, What is this then that is written, The stone which the builders rejected, the same is become the head of the corner?

18 Whosoever shall fall upon that stone shall be broken; but on whomsoever it shall fall, it will grind him to powder.

19 And the chief priests and the scribes the same hour sought to lay hands on him; and they feared the people: for they perceived that he had spoken this parable against them.

The Cornerstone Becomes the Stumbling Stone

This parable grows out of the nasty attitude the Pharisees display in Luke 20:1–8. Christ skillfully uses well-known incidents and familiar figures to expose the attitude of Israel toward the prophets God had sent to them in the past. All the prophets—even Moses—had suffered through their unbelief.

In parable format, Jesus Christ tells the sad history of Israel. His listeners know exactly what he is talking about. But their continual rejection of God does not seem to affect their hearts. They are ready to do just as their forefathers did (v. 19). This exposes the total failure of law and ritual as a link between God and man. And so Israel's history sounds a warning to all humanity: Such religion, no matter its variety—Christian, Jewish, Islamic, etc., subverts human morals. Such religious men are about to commit the crime of crimes.

1. In Acts 7:52, Stephen gave the council of Israel the same message as this parable. What was their response? (See verses 58–60.)

2. In 1 Thessalonians 1:15, Paul repeats this theme. In verse 16, whom else are the Jews opposing?

The apostle Peter echoes Luke 20:17–18 in evoking the rejected cornerstone (1 Peter 2:6–8). The head cornerstone of a masonry building is the most ornamental and honorable in the whole structure. Israel should elevate Christ to that position. Instead, they cast the stone to the ground where it becomes a stone of stumbling (v. 8). Peter personally saw them stumble over it. So, the builders of Israel have hurt themselves on Christ. But, it is important to note that they have not stumbled to fall. One day, "Out of Zion will come the Deliverer; he will banish ungodliness from Jacob (Romans 11:11, 26; Isaiah 59:20 NRSV).

3. According to Romans 11:30, what have we received because of Israel's disobedience?

4. Read Romans 11:11. What has come to the Gentiles through Israel's stumbling?

Day Sixty-Three

Luke 22:47–62

47 And while he yet spake, behold a multitude, and he that was called Judas, one of the twelve, went before them, and drew near unto Jesus to kiss him.

48 But Jesus said unto him, Judas, betrayest thou the Son of man with a kiss? . . .

51 And Jesus answered and said, Suffer ye thus far. And he touched his ear, and healed him.

52 Then Jesus said unto the chief priests, and captains of the temple, and the elders, which were come to him, Be ye come out, as against a thief, with swords and staves?

53 When I was daily with you in the temple, ye stretched forth no hands against me: but this is your hour, and the power of darkness.

54 Then took they him, and led him, and brought him into the high priest's house. And Peter followed afar off.

55 And when they had kindled a fire in the midst of the hall, and were set down together, Peter sat down among them.

56 But a certain maid beheld him as he sat by the fire, and earnestly looked upon him, and said, This man was also with him.

57 And he denied him, saying, Woman, I know him not.

58 And after a little while another saw him, and said, Thou art also of them. And Peter said, Man, I am not.

59 And about the space of one hour after another confidently affirmed, saying, Of a truth this fellow also was with him: for he is a Galilaean.

60 And Peter said, Man, I know not what thou sayest. And immediately, while he yet spake, the cock crew.

61 And the Lord turned, and looked upon Peter. And Peter remembered the word of the Lord, how he had said unto him, Before the cock crow, thou shalt deny me thrice.

62 And Peter went out, and wept bitterly.

Peter Is Sifted

It is evident that Judas would not have betrayed the Lord on his own. Only when Satan personally possesses him does he carry out such a shameful deed (Luke 22:3; John 13:2). This fact should help us adjust our judgment of him. Could any of Christ's disciples have done otherwise when under the control of God's adversary?

1. Read Matthew 27:3. What was Judas's response when he saw that Christ was condemned?

Both Judas's betrayal and Peter's denial of the Lord are the work of Satan. Judas is actually possessed by the enemy, while Peter is the object of an outward attack. He is not singled out for discipline because he was more selfish than the rest of the disciples. They all clamored for the highest place (Luke 9:46; 22:24). But, the Lord wants Peter to be the leading one among them. So, it is necessary for him to be truly humble (v. 26).

Earlier, the Lord had informed Peter, "Satan has asked to sift you as wheat" (v. 31). Farmers sift wheat to get rid of the chaff. This is also called threshing. So, Peter is sifted in the courtyard of the high priest to be purged of the chaff of self-importance. This frees him to exercise his excellent qualities in proclaiming the kingdom. However, the Lord limits Satan's claim on Peter (v. 32). The enemy is allowed to do only so much evil as will result in good. It is sobering to know that Satan had a hand in preparing Peter for his high place among the apostles. This shows that all satanic efforts are turned to God's advantage.

2. In Job 1:10–12 and 2:5, God gives Satan power over Job's life. In 5:5, how does God limit the Adversary? In 42:5, what is the result of Job's suffering?

Peter really intends to be loyal to his Lord. He does not run away but follows as closely as he dares, always keeping his Master in sight. It takes courage to enter into the courtyard of the chief priest. But what he sees there could not have inspired confidence. If they treat his Master in this way, what will they do to him? Suddenly Peter is afraid of a maid (vv. 57–57). However, from the moment Christ looks at Peter, he is a changed man (v. 61). Bitter self-reproach takes the place of boasting (v. 62).

Confidence in Christ replaces self-conceit. He has learned the lesson of true greatness. Then, he can speak with boldness to the very council that condemned his Lord (Acts 4:5–13).

3. What advice does Peter give to the believers in 1 Peter 5:6?

4. Read Job 5:11. What does God do for lowly people?

Answer Key to
Questions in Luke

Day Question

43. 1. Prepare the way of the Lord.
    2. In Christ, every one of God's promises are a "Yes."
    3. God will bless Abraham; His descendants will be as numerous as the stars in the sky and as the sand on the seashore; His descendants will take possession their enemies' cities; Through Abraham's offspring nations on earth will be blessed.

44. 1. The Spirit of wisdom and of understanding, the Spirit of counsel and of power, the Spirit of knowledge and of the fear of the Lord.
    2. He took the child and Mary and fled to Egypt.
    3. The child is appointed for the fall and rise of many in Israel. He is a sign to be opposed. A sword will pierce Mary's soul.

45. 1. "It is written."
    2. By humbling them, causing them to hunger, and feeding them with manna.
    3. He will hate the one, and love the other; or else he will hold to the one, and despise the other.
    4. Serpents destroyed them.

46. 1. Peter, Andrew, James, and John.
    2. "I will make you fish for men."
    3. They caught one hundred and fifty-three fish.
    4. No.

47. 1. Do no work on the Sabbath.
    2. On the Sabbath, the priests made a burnt offering of two lambs with a drink offering and a grain offering mixed with oil in addition to the regular burnt offering and drink offering.
    3. One enters the millennial rest by believing.

48. 1. Israel will weep over Christ.
    2. Paul persecuted the church of God. God's grace made him what he was.
    3. Grace abounds much more (see Romans 6:1).

49. 1. The waters are peoples, and multitudes and nations, and languages.
    2. In the evening, indicating the end of this age.
    3. Peace be with you.

50. 1. He would not entrust himself to them.
    2. "Far be it from you Lord; this shall not happen to you!" (NIV).
    3. It is hostile to God.

51. 1. Through the law, we become conscious of sin.
    2. People from Babylon, Cuthah, Avva, Hamath and Sepharvaim.
    3. They are cursed.
    4. Instead of "Love your neighbor," Christ taught, "Love your enemies."

52. 1. The finger of God.
    2. One thousand years.
    3. The evil one.

53. 1. A Savior.
    2. We are saved by grace through faith, which is the gift of God. Our works do not save us.
    3. They should be encouraging.

54. 1. The Pharisees prevented them from entering.
    2. The entire house [nation] of Israel.
    3. Repent and be baptized.
    4. God does not count our sins against us.

55. 1. He was sent to the lost sheep of the house of Israel.
    2. He lays down his life for the sheep.
    3. He has laid on him the iniquity of us all.
    4. They are the jewels adorning a bride.

56. 1. Their worship is made up only of rules taught by men.
    2. My dear son and child; God is deeply moved for him; God will have mercy on him.
    3. God redeemed his soul from going down to the pit.
    4. So grace might reign through righteousness to bring eternal life through Jesus Christ our Lord.

57. 1. We store up for ourselves the treasure of a good foundation for the future.
    2. In all that is good, right, and true.
    3. He becomes an enemy of God.

58. 1. Her maker is her husband.
    2. The bride of Christ.
    3. She had pride, excess of food, and prosperous ease but did not aid the poor and needy.
    4. He was proclaimed to the Jews in Jerusalem, Judea, Samaria, and to the ends of the earth.

59. 1. In the sun, and in the moon, and in the stars.
    2. The Son of Man suffers greatly, is rejected by Israel, killed, and resurrected.
    3. To be born in spirit in John fulfills the promise of the new spirit in Ezekiel.
    4. They were eating and drinking, marrying and giving in marriage.

60. 1. Make him an offering for sin (NRSV).
    2. Psalm 16 speaks of the resurrection of the Messiah.
    3. They call him a prophet. He calls himself the Messiah.

61. 1. Bear fruit worthy of repentance.
    2. They both had been forgiven much, so they loved the Lord greatly.
    3. Zacchaeus believed.

62. 1. They killed Stephen.
    2. They oppose everyone by attempting to keep Paul from bringing the gospel to the Gentiles.

3. Mercy (see Romans 11:31–32).

4. Salvation.

63. 1. Judas repented.

    2. Formerly, Job had only heard of God. But after his suffering at Satan's hand, he declared, "Now my eye sees you."

    3. "Humble yourselves, therefore, under God's mighty hand, that he may lift you up in due time" (NIV).

    4. God sets them on high (NRSV).

INTRODUCTION TO THE GOSPEL OF JOHN

In Matthew, Jesus is the king. Mark shows him as a servant. Luke impresses us with his humanity. But John reveals his divine relationship as God's Son. Matthew and Luke give Jesus' human genealogies. Mark's lowly servant has no pedigree. But John is far above genealogies. He unveils that our Lord existed as the Word with God long before he came in the flesh (John 1:1).

This account of Christ's life was not written until the end of the first century, after the apostolic ministry had ended. Possibly none of the other apostles even saw it. They never used it in the period recorded in the book of Acts. For this reason, it especially applies to the coming kingdom era. Unlike the other three accounts, it suggests Christ's rejection in its first chapter (1:11). There also, it refers to Christ as the Lamb of God (v. 29), indicating his crucifixion before his ministry has even begun. Immediately it tells of a wedding feast (2:1), a preview of the marriage of the Lamb (Revelation 19:9). And it gives a series of seven signs, all of which find their fulfillment in the kingdom age.

Each of the seven signs exhibits Jesus as the incarnate Word. Unlike other accounts, there is no personal contact or action in these events. He simply speaks, and the miracle is done. He accomplished these things by his word because of what he is. He speaks, and water becomes wine (2:7), a dead boy lives (4:50), and a sick man is healed (5:8). At his word, five thousand people are fed (6:11), his disciples are rescued at sea (6:20), a blind man is given sight (9:7), and Lazarus is raised from the dead (11:43).

John's account follows the pattern of the two phases of Christ's life: "He came out from God and is going away to God" (13:3). In the beginning, he is with God. Then he comes in the flesh as the divine expression—the Word—to minister to Israel. But his own people reject Him (12:37). The balance of the book is occupied with his journey back to God.

Day Sixty-Four

John 1:19–31

19 And this is the record of John, when the Jews sent priests and Levites from Jerusalem to ask him, Who art thou?

20 And he confessed, and denied not; but confessed, I am not the Christ.

21 And they asked him, What then? Art thou Elias? And he saith, I am not. Art thou that prophet? And he answered, No.

22 Then said they unto him, Who art thou? that we may give an answer to them that sent us. What sayest thou of thyself?

23 He said, I am the voice of one crying in the wilderness, Make straight the way of the Lord, as said the prophet Esaias.

24 And they which were sent were of the Pharisees.

25 And they asked him, and said unto him, Why baptizest thou then, if thou be not that Christ, nor Elias, neither that prophet?

26 John answered them, saying, I baptize with water: but there standeth one among you, whom ye know not;

27 He it is, who coming after me is preferred before me, whose shoe's latchet I am not worthy to unloose.

28 These things were done in Bethabara beyond Jordan, where John was baptizing.

29 The next day John seeth Jesus coming unto him, and saith, Behold the Lamb of God, which taketh away the sin of the world.

30 This is he of whom I said, After me cometh a man which is preferred before me: for he was before me.

31 And I knew him not: but that he should be made manifest to Israel, therefore am I come baptizing with water.

The Lamb of God

The lamb was freely used in the sacrifices prescribed by Moses in the Hebrew Scriptures. On seven different occasions, a lamb is used to depict the sacrificial work of the Messiah. Four times, it is used for negative purposes; three ordinances describe its use on the positive side. John's account of the Lord's life reflects this. Two times in two days, John the

Baptist points out God's Lamb. He first highlights the Lamb who takes away sin (John 1:29):

• A Lamb was slain at the Passover (Exodus13:3).

• It was used as a sin offering (Leviticus 4:32).

• It was a guilt offering (Leviticus 5:6).

• A lamb was prescribed for the cleansing of a leper (Leviticus 14:12).

   1. According to Leviticus 5:7, what animals can one offer if a lamb is too expensive? (See Matthew 3:16.)

John speaks with two of his disciples the second time he points out the Lamb (John 1:36). This shows that the Lamb of God is not only for sinners but also for saints. So Moses taught that a lamb be used for worship and communion with God:

• Every morning and evening a lamb was an ascending offering (Exodus 29:38–39).

• It was used as a peace offering (Leviticus 3:7).

• A Lamb was presented with the wave offering (Leviticus 14:24).

But none of these lambs could take away the sin of the whole world as does Jesus Christ, the Lamb of God.

   2. When John pointed out the Lamb of God to his disciples, what did they do first (John 1:36–37)?

Christ ministered for approximately four years. These point to the four days during which the Passover lamb was kept before it could be offered (Exodus 12:2–6). In his ministry, the Lord displayed his perfection to the world. Not a blemish was found in him. No wonder John's disciples left him and followed Jesus Christ.

   3. Compare Matthew 27:31 with Isaiah 53:7. How was the soldiers' treatment of Jesus similar to that of a lamb?

Day Sixty-Five

John 2:13–25

13 And the Jews' passover was at hand, and Jesus went up to Jerusalem.

14 And found in the temple those that sold oxen and sheep and doves, and the changers of money sitting:

15 And when he had made a scourge of small cords, he drove them all out of the temple, and the sheep, and the oxen; and poured out the changers' money, and overthrew the tables;

16 And said unto them that sold doves, Take these things hence; make not my Father's house an house of merchandise.

17 And his disciples remembered that it was written, The zeal of thine house hath eaten me up.

18 Then answered the Jews and said unto him, What sign shewest thou unto us, seeing that thou doest these things?

19 Jesus answered and said unto them, Destroy this temple, and in three days I will raise it up.

20 Then said the Jews, Forty and six years was this temple in building, and wilt thou rear it up in three days?

21 But he spake of the temple of his body.

22 When therefore he was risen from the dead, his disciples remembered that he had said this unto them; and they believed the scripture, and the word which Jesus had said.

23 Now when he was in Jerusalem at the passover, in the feast day, many believed in his name, when they saw the miracles which he did.

24 But Jesus did not commit himself unto them, because he knew all men,

25 And needed not that any should testify of man: for he knew what was in man.

Christ's Omniscience

Omniscience is the state of having infinite knowledge. This belongs to Jesus Christ as the Son of God and is especially evident in John's gospel. No matter our social class or spiritual condition, Christ knows all hearts:

- He sees that Nathaniel is guileless (1:47).

- The applause of the crowd does not blind Him to their motives (2:24–25).

- He knows that Nicodemus, Israel's teacher, is ignorant (John 3:10).

- The woman of Samaria recognizes that he knows all her past (4:29).

- The impotent man at Bethesda learns that Christ fully understands his failure (5:6).

- He knows the crowd has no hunger for spiritual food (6:34–36).

- Judas's treachery is known from the very first (13:11).

- The Lord recognizes Peter to be a fond and faithful spiritual friend (13:37; 21:17).

- He is aware of all things (16:30).

1. Read John 6:64. Does the Lord know beforehand who will not believe in him?

2. Does Jesus know that Judas will betray him? (See John 6:64.)

Our character, conduct, condition, and motives are transparent to the Lord's view. This is why Jesus does not commit himself to the crowd (John 2:24–25). Their faith is captured by miracles, not Messiah. He knows the hearts of those men and women and does not entrust himself to faith found in signs.

"Jesus knew that the Father had put all things under his power, and that he had come from God and was returning to God" (13:3). This marvelous passage simultaneously reveals Christ's omniscience and humility. First is his high place in relation to the world—all is in his hands since he came from God. This dignity and power entitle him to the highest esteem. Nonetheless, he stoops to the lowest humility as he is crucified upon his return to God.

3. Read Deuteronomy 31:20–21. What does God know about Israel before they enter the Good Land?

DAY SIXTY-SIX

John 3:23–30

23 And John also was baptizing in Aenon near to Salim, because there was much water there: and they came, and were baptized.

24 For John was not yet cast into prison.

25 Then there arose a question between some of John's disciples and the Jews about purifying.

26 And they came unto John, and said unto him, Rabbi, he that was with thee beyond Jordan, to whom thou barest witness, behold, the same baptizeth, and all men come to him.

27 John answered and said, A man can receive nothing, except it be given him from heaven.

28 Ye yourselves bear me witness, that I said, I am not the Christ, but that I am sent before him.

29 He that hath the bride is the bridegroom: but the friend of the bridegroom, which standeth and heareth him, rejoiceth greatly because of the bridegroom's voice: this my joy therefore is fulfilled.

30 He must increase, but I must decrease.

The Bridegroom and the Bride

The Old Testament depicts Israel as the bride or wife of God. Isaiah informed the nation, "Your maker is your husband" (54:5 NRSV). Jeremiah began his prophecy to Israel in this way: "Thus says the Lord: I remember the devotion of your youth, your love as a bride" (2:2).

1. Read Jeremiah 31:32. What was God's relationship with Israel when they were rescued from Egypt?

2. In Jeremiah 3:8, what did God do because of Israel's unfaithfulness?

Tragically, though she was a bride dressed in jewels (Ezekiel 16:11–13), Israel became a whore because of idolatry (vv. 15–17). The girl forgot her ornaments, the bride her attire (Jeremiah 2:32). Yet, at the beginning of John's gospel, the bride and the divine bridegroom are seen afresh. God promised not to be angry forever (Jeremiah 3:12), and so the Messiah has come to bring God's children to Zion (v. 14). The joy of John the Baptist, the friend of the bridegroom and Israel's last prophet, is fulfilled. He declares, "He who has the bride is the bridegroom" (John 3:29). In this chapter, we stand at the threshold of the wedding supper of the Lamb (Luke 14:15; Revelation 19:9).

3. Read Hosea 3:1–5. When will Israel return to her husband? (See verse 5.)

John chapter 2 begins with a wedding supper. Dominating this scene are six large stone jars containing twenty or thirty gallons of water (John 2:6). These represent the Law, which deadened the gladness of the bride and her bridegroom. But Christ changes this water into wine. One hundred eighty gallons of wine is a rich image of the joy that will come with Christ in his kingdom.

4. In Revelation 21:2, John sees "the holy city, the new Jerusalem, coming down out of heaven from God" (NRSV). What is this city likened to?

Day Sixty-Seven

John 4:4–15

4 And he must needs go through Samaria.

5 Then cometh he to a city of Samaria, which is called Sychar, near to the parcel of ground that Jacob gave to his son Joseph.

6 Now Jacob's well was there. Jesus therefore, being wearied with his journey, sat thus on the well: and it was about the sixth hour.

7 There cometh a woman of Samaria to draw water: Jesus saith unto her, Give me to drink.

8 (For his disciples were gone away unto the city to buy meat.)

9 Then saith the woman of Samaria unto him, How is it that thou, being a Jew, askest drink of me, which am a woman of Samaria? for the Jews have no dealings with the Samaritans.

10 Jesus answered and said unto her, If thou knewest the gift of God, and who it is that saith to thee, Give me to drink; thou wouldest have asked of him, and he would have given thee living water.

11 The woman saith unto him, Sir, thou hast nothing to draw with, and the well is deep: from whence then hast thou that living water?

12 Art thou greater than our father Jacob, which gave us the well, and drank thereof himself, and his children, and his cattle?

13 Jesus answered and said unto her, Whosoever drinketh of this water shall thirst again:

14 But whosoever drinketh of the water that I shall give him shall never thirst; but the water that I shall give him shall be in him a well of water springing up into everlasting life.

15 The woman saith unto him, Sir, give me this water, that I thirst not, neither come hither to draw.

The Well of Living Water

Just as physical life is dependent on water, the Spirit and word of God sustain spiritual life. We in modern America are accustomed to an ample supply of water. This weakens the force of the Lord's promise that "the water that I shall give him shall be in him a well of water springing up into everlasting life" (John 4:14).

In the arid Middle East, a thirsty traveler knew the delight of a drink of pure water. There, a water seller carried a porous clay jar of water that kept its contents cool by evaporation. Rattling cups accompanied his shout, "Ho, everyone who thirsts, come to the waters!" (Isaiah 55:1). A spring or well was a prized possession that cost enormous labor. A town like the one where Jesus rested depended on such a spring for its existence.

1. In John 7:37–38, Jesus cries out like a water seller. What is his promise in verse 38?

2. What does this promise refer to? (See verse 39.)

Jesus is resting at Jacob's spring. This was a deep well where there was no windlass or bucket. Travelers carried their own long leather buckets. But the Lord and his disciples were not so equipped. This gave him a good excuse to break from the strict etiquette of the day that prevented a man from speaking to a strange woman.

The physical figure of a well falls short of the reality of the Spirit, which is like an artesian spring that bubbles up and overflows with blessing to all. With it, the Samaritan woman has no need of a bucket to draw out a limited supply. She has no need to walk a long distance lugging a water jar. The Spirit is within her always, flowing out to others (John 4:28–30).

3. In John 6:35, what satisfies a person's spiritual thirst?

Day Sixty-Eight

John 4:46–54

46 So Jesus came again into Cana of Galilee, where he made the water wine. And there was a certain nobleman, whose son was sick at Capernaum.

47 When he heard that Jesus was come out of Judaea into Galilee, he went unto him, and besought him that he would come down, and heal his son: for he was at the point of death.

48 Then said Jesus unto him, Except ye see signs and wonders, ye will not believe.

49 The nobleman saith unto him, Sir, come down ere my child die.

50 Jesus saith unto him, Go thy way; thy son liveth. And the man believed the word that Jesus had spoken unto him, and he went his way.

51 And as he was now going down, his servants met him, and told him, saying, Thy son liveth.

52 Then enquired he of them the hour when he began to amend. And they said unto him, Yesterday at the seventh hour the fever left him.

53 So the father knew that it was at the same hour, in the which Jesus said unto him, Thy son liveth: and himself believed, and his whole house.

54 This is again the second miracle that Jesus did, when he was come out of Judaea into Galilee.

The Healing of the Nations

In the first sign at Cana, water turned to wine (John 2:9). This signifies the blessing of Israel in the kingdom. The second sign, also at Cana, is concerned with the coming kingdom as well. It foreshadows the healing of the nations.

Human government has brought a fever on the world's nations as seen in the sickness of the official's son (John 4:52). The last century saw the hottest of all wars that ended in atomic holocaust. The chill of a cold war followed, and today the world suffers from a low-grade fever of oppression. Terrorism has introduced a dread of death to the nations like that of the official himself (v. 49). This will be far worse at the time of the end.

1. Revelation 6:1–8 shows the opening of the first four seals at the end of this age. In verse 8, what is the result of this?

This fever cannot be cured by human therapy. The coming of Christ is the cure (John 4:49). Notice the hour in which the boy was healed (v. 52). The seventh hour suggests the time of the opening of the seventh seal (Revelation 8:1), which culminates in the sounding of the seventh trumpet (11:15).

2. Read Revelation 11:15. What results from the sounding of the seventh trumpet?

Christ will ease the pain and unrest that now possess the world. He will change its fever into a thousand years of peace (Revelation 20:4). Just as he fearful official prays, "Sir, come down!" (John 4:49), believers today should pray with the same urgency, "Come, Lord Jesus!" (Revelation 22:20).

The Lord, however, does not personally visit the official's son, but heals him at a distance. Christ will deal with the nations in the millennial era in the same way. Their blessing comes through Israel (Romans 9:4–5).

3. In Revelation 22:2, what heals the nations?

Day Sixty-Nine

John 6:1–14

1 After these things Jesus went over the sea of Galilee, which is the sea of Tiberias.

2 And a great multitude followed him, because they saw his miracles which he did on them that were diseased.

3 And Jesus went up into a mountain, and there he sat with his disciples.

4 And the passover, a feast of the Jews, was nigh.

5 When Jesus then lifted up his eyes, and saw a great company come unto him, he saith unto Philip, Whence shall we buy bread, that these may eat?

6 And this he said to prove him: for he himself knew what he would do.

7 Philip answered him, Two hundred pennyworth of bread is not sufficient for them, that every one of them may take a little.

8 One of his disciples, Andrew, Simon Peter's brother, saith unto him,

9 There is a lad here, which hath five barley loaves, and two small fishes: but what are they among so many?

10 And Jesus said, Make the men sit down. Now there was much grass in the place. So the men sat down, in number about five thousand.

11 And Jesus took the loaves; and when he had given thanks, he distributed to the disciples, and the disciples to them that were set down; and likewise of the fishes as much as they would.

12 When they were filled, he said unto his disciples, Gather up the fragments that remain, that nothing be lost.

13 Therefore they gathered them together, and filled twelve baskets with the fragments of the five barley loaves, which remained over and above unto them that had eaten.

14 Then those men, when they had seen the miracle that Jesus did, said, This is of a truth that prophet that should come into the world.

The Earth Is Filled with the Knowledge of the Lord

This is the fourth sign in John's gospel. The first illustrates Israel's joy in the coming kingdom (2:1–11). The second tells of the healing of the nations (4:46–54). The third shows the Messiah as the source of Israel's healing (5:2–18). The fourth deals with the world's nourishment.

Christ is the life of the world, the true bread (John 6:35). The five thousand hungry people picture mankind, which is far from food (v. 5). They only have enough food for five people (v. 9). The lack is a thousand-fold showing the great spiritual famine that currently ravages the earth.

1. According to Matthew 4:4, what is the true nourishment of mankind?

2. In Isaiah 11:9, what will fill the earth in the kingdom?

A full stomach alone cannot sustain the world. The head and heart must be fed by the knowledge of God. This feeding of the multitude is a sign of Christ's presence in the kingdom when the knowledge of the Lord will be a thousand times what it is today.

The less man can do, the more God can provide. At another time, the Lord fed four thousand people (Matthew 15:32–38; Mark 8:1–9). There, seven loaves and some fish were used to feed the multitudes and they gathered seven baskets full of leftovers. Here, five loaves and two fish are distributed among five thousand. Yet after feeding a larger number with a smaller portion, there is a larger surplus. Twelve large full baskets remain (John 6:13). Clearly, the less there is of human help, the greater is God's grace. So at the end of this age, man's extreme famine is turned into the feast of God's kingdom. That kingdom is not food and drink (Romans 14:17), which man can provide. Rather, in the kingdom, all will know God, from the least to the greatest (Jeremiah 31:34).

3. Read 2 Corinthians 12:9. What perfects God's grace?

Day Seventy

John 6:26–35

26 Jesus answered them and said, Verily, verily, I say unto you, Ye seek me, not because ye saw the miracles, but because ye did eat of the loaves, and were filled.

27 Labour not for the meat which perisheth, but for that meat which endureth unto everlasting life, which the Son of man shall give unto you: for him hath God the Father sealed.

28 Then said they unto him, What shall we do, that we might work the works of God?

29 Jesus answered and said unto them, This is the work of God, that ye believe on him whom he hath sent.

30 They said therefore unto him, What sign shewest thou then, that we may see, and believe thee? what dost thou work?

31 Our fathers did eat manna in the desert; as it is written, He gave them bread from heaven to eat.

32 Then Jesus said unto them, Verily, verily, I say unto you, Moses gave you not that bread from heaven; but my Father giveth you the true bread from heaven.

33 For the bread of God is he which cometh down from heaven, and giveth life unto the world.

34 Then said they unto him, Lord, evermore give us this bread.

35 And Jesus said unto them, I am the bread of life: he that cometh to me shall never hunger; and he that believeth on me shall never thirst.

The Bread of Life

The miracle of feeding the five thousand brings the Lord to the highest pitch of his popularity. Yet as he fills the people with food, they are too blind to see the meaning of this. When he explains it, they stop following him (John 6:66). They are there to be filled with food and care nothing for the spiritual sustenance that it represents. They want food but need faith. They do not read this sign and recognize the Son of God. Instead, they ask him for a sign, though he has just given them one (6:30). They further display their blindness by reminding Christ of the manna that God gave in the wilderness (Psalm 78:23–25). The bread of life is there with them, yet they ask for a sign like the one Moses gave their ancestors.

1. Read Exodus 16:2–4. Why did God send manna to Israel?

2. In John 6:32–35, what does Jesus indicate he is?

The crowd has been freely fed. They've heard that God will give them the true bread (John 6:27). One would expect they'd understand that there is no price on God's gifts. But instead of gratefully receiving the bread of life, they try to strike a bargain with God (v. 28). Their pride demands they do something to earn what God wants to freely give. Faith, not works, is what God desires of us (v. 35).

3. Read John 6:35. How does one eat the bread of life?

In John's gospel, Jesus Christ is displayed as the Word (1:1). This book is given that we can learn to not live by bread alone, but by every word that proceeds out of God's mouth (Luke 4:4; Deuteronomy 8:3). This is why John makes so much of eating and drinking.

DAY SEVENTY-ONE

John 7:28–46

28 Then cried Jesus in the temple as he taught, saying, Ye both know me, and ye know whence I am: and I am not come of myself, but he that sent me is true, whom ye know not.

29 But I know him: for I am from him, and he hath sent me.

30 Then they sought to take him: but no man laid hands on him, because his hour was not yet come.

31 And many of the people believed on him, and said, When Christ cometh, will he do more miracles than these which this man hath done?

32 The Pharisees heard that the people murmured such things concerning him; and the Pharisees and the chief priests sent officers to take him. . . .

37 In the last day, that great day of the feast, Jesus stood and cried, saying, If any man thirst, let him come unto me, and drink.

38 He that believeth on me, as the scripture hath said, out of his belly shall flow rivers of living water.

39 (But this spake he of the Spirit, which they that believe on him should receive: for the Holy Ghost was not yet given; because that Jesus was not yet glorified.)

40 Many of the people therefore, when they heard this saying, said, Of a truth this is the Prophet.

41 Others said, This is the Christ. But some said, Shall Christ come out of Galilee?

42 Hath not the scripture said, That Christ cometh of the seed of David, and out of the town of Bethlehem, where David was?

43 So there was a division among the people because of him.

44 And some of them would have taken him; but no man laid hands on him.

45 Then came the officers to the chief priests and Pharisees; and they said unto them, Why have ye not brought him?

46 The officers answered, Never man spake like this man.

The Arresting Words of Christ

The scene depicted in John 7:14–52 shows the utter futility of human efforts to frustrate God's plans. It was God's definite counsel that Christ be slain (Acts 2:23). The leaders of Israel are eager to do this. But the feast of Tabernacles is not the correct time for this sacrifice. So the Lord boldly enters the temple, which is the stronghold of his enemies.

1. Read Acts 2:23. How was Jesus Christ's death accomplished?

The Pharisees send the temple police to arrest the Lord (John 7:32). But he is not disturbed. Instead, he calmly gives an outline of what will happen to him in the near future (vv. 33–34). It is still six months until the Passover, and he knows they cannot arrest him until then. So, he says, "I will be with you a little while longer." He makes it clear that they alone cannot take him even at the proper time. His permission, not their power, accomplishes his arrest. He describes his betrayal, arrest, and crucifixion in this way: "Then I am going to him who sent me." This is his choice.

2. According to John 16:28, where did Christ come from, and where was he going?

Throughout John's account of Christ's life, he is seen as the Word become flesh (1:1, 14). The testimony of the deputies is a notable tribute to the celestial nature of his words. The deputies seem to be simply overwhelmed by them. It is not a handsome face or imposing figure that captures them (Isaiah 53:2); his speech does the job. Christ so arrests the officers that they can only report : "Never has anyone spoken like this!" (7:46).

3. In John 6:66–68, the twelve disciples did not walk out on the Lord. Why not?

Day Seventy-Two

John 8:49–59

49 Jesus answered, I have not a devil; but I honour my Father, and ye do dishonour me.

50 And I seek not mine own glory: there is one that seeketh and judgeth.

51 Verily, verily, I say unto you, If a man keep my saying, he shall never see death.

52 Then said the Jews unto him, Now we know that thou hast a devil. Abraham is dead, and the prophets; and thou sayest, If a man keep my saying, he shall never taste of death.

53 Art thou greater than our father Abraham, which is dead? and the prophets are dead: whom makest thou thyself?

54 Jesus answered, If I honour myself, my honour is nothing: it is my Father that honoureth me; of whom ye say, that he is your God:

55 Yet ye have not known him; but I know him: and if I should say, I know him not, I shall be a liar like unto you: but I know him, and keep his saying.

56 Your father Abraham rejoiced to see my day: and he saw it, and was glad.

57 Then said the Jews unto him, Thou art not yet fifty years old, and hast thou seen Abraham?

58 Jesus said unto them, Verily, verily, I say unto you, Before Abraham was, I am.

59 Then took they up stones to cast at him: but Jesus hid himself, and went out of the temple, going through the midst of them, and so passed by.

Christ from the Beginning to the Consummation

The Word was in the beginning with God long before Abraham was born (John 1:1). Here he reveals this to the Pharisees: "Before Abraham was, I am" (8:58). Everything came into being through the Word, including Abraham himself (1:3). The existence of all things is based on Christ as the Word of God while creation is connected with Christ as the image of God (Colossians 1:15–17). The reason for this is that creation provides a domain where God can be revealed (the image of God) and expressed (the Word of God).

In other words, sounds without ears are nothing. Sights without eyes are useless. God wants to be known. This is the reason for Jesus Christ who reveals the invisible God to creation.

1. Read John 14:8–9. How does one see the Father?

Formerly, no human could see God and live (Exodus 33:20). However, "In these last days he has spoken to us by a Son" (Hebrews 1:2 NRSV) who is "the reflection of God's glory and the exact imprint of God's very being" (v. 3). This occurred after Christ emptied himself to be in the likeness of humanity (Philippians 2:7).

2. Read Philippians 2:6–7. When Christ emptied himself of the form of God, what did he become?

Some say the words of Philippians 2:6–11 are the lyrics to an early hymn. These verses provide a summary of Christ's service and suffering in an enormous sweep that takes in the whole universe and all the eons from the beginning to the consummation:

• From the beginning, Christ was in the form of God above the heavens (v. 6).

• He voluntarily descended from the highest to the lowest place (v. 7).

• Furthermore, he humbled himself under the curse of the cross to become lower than the low (v. 8).

• God has been engaged in Christ's exaltation since the resurrection (v. 9).

• Many celestial powers are currently subject to him (1 Peter 3:22).

• When he comes again, the earth will be added to his domain (Revelation 11:15).

• Finally, the whole universe will be reconciled to God by the blood of his cross (Colossians 1:20).

- And every heart will be subdued at the consummation (1 Corinthians 15:28).

Then, as Jesus (his name in humiliation), he will be exalted to the highest place for God the Father's glory and the lowest will again become the highest (Philippians 2:9–11).

3. Read Colossians 1:20. What is reconciled to God by the blood of the cross?

4. 1 Corinthians 15:28 describes the consummation of all things. What is this consummation?

DAY SEVENTY-THREE

John 9:1–12

1 And as Jesus passed by, he saw a man which was blind from his birth.

2 And his disciples asked him, saying, Master, who did sin, this man, or his parents, that he was born blind?

3 Jesus answered, Neither hath this man sinned, nor his parents: but that the works of God should be made manifest in him.

4 I must work the works of him that sent me, while it is day: the night cometh, when no man can work.

5 As long as I am in the world, I am the light of the world.

6 When he had thus spoken, he spat on the ground, and made clay of the spittle, and he anointed the eyes of the blind man with the clay,

7 And said unto him, Go, wash in the pool of Siloam, (which is by interpretation, Sent.) He went his way therefore, and washed, and came seeing.

8 The neighbours therefore, and they which before had seen him that he was blind, said, Is not this he that sat and begged?

9 Some said, This is he: others said, He is like him: but he said, I am he.

10 Therefore said they unto him, How were thine eyes opened?

11 He answered and said, A man that is called Jesus made clay, and anointed mine eyes, and said unto me, Go to the pool of Siloam, and wash: and I went and washed, and I received sight.

12 Then said they unto him, Where is he? He said, I know not.

The Philosophy of Sin (2)

The disciples ask a good question: "Why was this man born blind?" (John 9:2). Then as now, it was taken for granted that all evil comes from sin and that everyone is responsible for his own condition. But evil and sin are not outside of "the purpose of the one who accomplishes all things according to his counsel and will" (Ephesians 1:11). This man's case is a concrete example of the philosophy of sin (see day forty-eight, page 128). That is, though hateful in itself, sin's ultimate effect is to reveal God's love.

1. According to Romans 5:20, what happens when sin increases?

The man was blind so he could recover his sight and reveal God's gracious work (John 9:3). This is ultimately true of all evil and all sin that we see in ourselves and in the world. Satan did not plant the tree of the knowledge of good and evil in the Garden of Eden (Genesis 2:8–9). This was done by God, "according to his counsel and will." Adam lived there in innocence. He was ignorant of evil and did not know good, either. He could not appreciate what God had done for him in placing him in the pristine garden. The only way he could know God's goodness was to eat of the tree, which also gave the knowledge of evil. The knowledge of good and that of evil are inseparable.

By planting that tree, God introduced evil into the world to reveal his marvelous qualities, which would otherwise have been unknown. In Christ, God copes with evil, and when its mission has been accomplished, removes it.

2. 1 Corinthians 15:42 says that all die in Adam. According to this verse, who are made alive in Christ?

3. In 1 Corinthians 15:26, what is the last enemy to be destroyed?

The philosophy of sin is seen in the story of the two sons in Luke 15:11–32 (see day fifty-six, page 147.) There, the elder son illustrates right living and law keeping. But his behavior, even if sincere and true, does not allow the Father a chance to reveal his love. The debauchery and decadence of the prodigal son, however, reveal the Father's unconditional love: "This son of mine was dead and is alive again; he was lost and is found" (Luke 15:24 NRSV).

Evil and sin are temporary, though their memory will never pass away. This will always remain as the black background for the brightness of God's goodness and grace. Without it, God's heart of love would remain hidden. Evil and sin are not eternal. If they were, their shadow would forever darken the character of God. Sin will be removed at the conclusion of the ages (Hebrews 9:26–28).

4. In Revelation 20:14, what eventually becomes of death before the coming of the New Jerusalem?

The question is, "Who sinned, this man or his parents, that he was born blind?" (John 9:2 NRSV). It is useless to blame our parents for our sin. They also inherited it. Its lineage descends through the generations to Adam himself. Even Adam pointed to Eve, and Eve blamed the serpent as the three of them gathered with God in the shadow of the tree of the knowledge of good and evil (Genesis 3:12–13). Then, the works of God began to be manifested (John 9:3).

Day Seventy-Four

John 9:13–25

13 They brought to the Pharisees him that aforetime was blind.

14 And it was the sabbath day when Jesus made the clay, and opened his eyes.

15 Then again the Pharisees also asked him how he had received his sight. He said unto them, He put clay upon mine eyes, and I washed, and do see.

16 Therefore said some of the Pharisees, This man is not of God, because he keepeth not the sabbath day. Others said, How can a man that is a sinner do such miracles? And there was a division among them.

17 They say unto the blind man again, What sayest thou of him, that he hath opened thine eyes? He said, He is a prophet.

18 But the Jews did not believe concerning him, that he had been blind, and received his sight, until they called the parents of him that had received his sight. . . .

20 His parents answered them and said, We know that this is our son, and that he was born blind:

21 But by what means he now seeth, we know not; or who hath opened his eyes, we know not: he is of age; ask him: he shall speak for himself.

22 These words spake his parents, because they feared the Jews: for the Jews had agreed already, that if any man did confess that he was Christ, he should be put out of the synagogue.

23 Therefore said his parents, He is of age; ask him.

24 Then again called they the man that was blind, and said unto him, Give God the praise: we know that this man is a sinner.

25 He answered and said, Whether he be a sinner or no, I know not: one thing I know, that, whereas I was blind, now I see.

Washing in Siloam

The blind man represents Israel. Why were Christ's countrymen blinded to his identity? Paul answers this question in Romans: Blindness caused Israel to refuse her Messiah. This made it possible for God to pour out the riches of grace on the Gentiles (11:11–12). When this has been accomplished, God will save Israel with a great salvation (vv. 25–27). Therefore, "God has imprisoned all in disobedience so that he may be merciful to all" (v. 32).

1. Read Matthew 13:13. Why did the Lord speak in parables?

Oddly enough, before he heals the blind man, the Lord increases his blindness by covering his eyes with mud. This corresponds with God's treatment of Israel. When the Son began his ministry, he found the nation blind to him. Instead of immediately healing them, he fulfilled the saying of Isaiah, "He has blinded their eyes and hardened their heart so that they might not look with their eyes and understand with their heart and turn—and I would heal them" (John 12:40; Isaiah 6:10).

The blind man, with mud on his eyes, was sent to the pool of Siloam to wash (9:7). The word *Siloam* means "sent" or "commissioned." When he was among them, Jesus Christ often referred to himself as the one whom God sent (8:42; 10:36, etc.). When the Lord appears in glory, Israel will look upon the one whom they have pierced (Zechariah 12:10). That day, they wash in Siloam and see that God has commissioned Christ for their blessing. This is their spiritual healing and like the blind man they will realize, "If this man were not from God, he could do nothing" (John 9:33).

2. Compare Zechariah 12:10 with John 19:34–37. When was Christ pierced?

3. Read John 9:35–41. What did the blind man do when he recognized the Lord?

4. In John 9:40–41, what was the Pharisees' sin?

DAY SEVENTY-FIVE

John 10:1–15

1 Verily, verily, I say unto you, He that entereth not by the door into the sheepfold, but climbeth up some other way, the same is a thief and a robber.

2 But he that entereth in by the door is the shepherd of the sheep.

3 To him the porter openeth; and the sheep hear his voice: and he calleth his own sheep by name, and leadeth them out. 4 And when he putteth forth his own sheep, he goeth before them, and the sheep follow him: for they know his voice.

5 And a stranger will they not follow, but will flee from him: for they know not the voice of strangers. . . .

7 Then said Jesus unto them again, Verily, verily, I say unto you, I am the door of the sheep.

8 All that ever came before me are thieves and robbers: but the sheep did not hear them.

9 I am the door: by me if any man enter in, he shall be saved, and shall go in and out, and find pasture.

10 The thief cometh not, but for to steal, and to kill, and to destroy: I am come that they might have life, and that they might have it more abundantly.

11 I am the good shepherd: the good shepherd giveth his life for the sheep.

12 But he that is an hireling, and not the shepherd, whose own the sheep are not, seeth the wolf coming, and leaveth the sheep, and fleeth: and the wolf catcheth them, and scattereth the sheep.

13 The hireling fleeth, because he is an hireling, and careth not for the sheep.

14 I am the good shepherd, and know my sheep, and am known of mine.

15 As the Father knoweth me, even so know I the Father: and I lay down my life for the sheep.

The Great Shepherd of the Sheep

In first-century Israel, a sheepfold was an enclosure created by a wall of rough stones about three feet wide at the base and tapering four to eight feet to the top. A narrow opening in this formed the entrance. There was no gate or door. The shepherd blocked the entrance at night with his body. He, himself, was the door that protected the sheep (John 10:7).

1. In 1 Samuel 17:36, what qualified David to kill Goliath?

These sheep runs were often in wild areas—the haunts of Bedouin robbers and wild animals. To protect his sheep, the shepherd had a stout club or rod about two feet long, with a large knob on one end studded with iron nails. The shepherd also had a crook or staff with which to guide his sheep.

2. In Psalm 23:4, what is a comfort to the psalmist?

The Psalms describe Israel as "the people of his pasture and the sheep of his hand" (95:7). Isaiah describes God as a tender shepherd of Israel (40:11). Jeremiah speaks woe to the spiritual shepherds of Israel and foretells the return of the scattered flock (23:1–4). Ezekiel speaks at length against Israel's spiritual shepherds (34:1–24). Finally, Jesus Christ uses the same metaphor, announcing himself as Israel's true shepherd and commissioning Peter to feed his sheep (John 21:16).

3. Read 1 Peter 5:1–2. What does Peter instruct the elders to do?

The figure of a shepherd with his sheep is particularly suited to the coming kingdom. There Christ, the true king, is a shepherd feeding and defending Israel. "The Lamb at the center of the throne will be their shepherd; he will lead them to springs of living water" (Revelation 7:17).

4. In crucifixion, the shepherd gave his life for the sheep (John 10:11). According to Hebrews 13:20–21, what does he do in resurrection?

Day Seventy-Six

John 11:1–15

1 Now a certain man was sick, named Lazarus, of Bethany, the town of Mary and her sister Martha.

2 (It was that Mary which anointed the Lord with ointment, and wiped his feet with her hair, whose brother Lazarus was sick.)

3 Therefore his sisters sent unto him, saying, Lord, behold, he whom thou lovest is sick.

4 When Jesus heard that, he said, This sickness is not unto death, but for the glory of God, that the Son of God might be glorified thereby.

5 Now Jesus loved Martha, and her sister, and Lazarus.

6 When he had heard therefore that he was sick, he abode two days still in the same place where he was.

7 Then after that saith he to his disciples, Let us go into Judaea again.

8 His disciples say unto him, Master, the Jews of late sought to stone thee; and goest thou thither again?

9 Jesus answered, Are there not twelve hours in the day? If any man walk in the day, he stumbleth not, because he seeth the light of this world.

10 But if a man walk in the night, he stumbleth, because there is no light in him.

11 These things said he: and after that he saith unto them, Our friend Lazarus sleepeth; but I go, that I may awake him out of sleep.

12 Then said his disciples, Lord, if he sleep, he shall do well.

13 Howbeit Jesus spake of his death: but they thought that he had spoken of taking of rest in sleep.

14 Then said Jesus unto them plainly, Lazarus is dead.

15 And I am glad for your sakes that I was not there, to the intent ye may believe; nevertheless let us go unto him.

"Lazarus Is Sleeping"

Sleep is the favorite figure for death in the scriptures. Here in John 11, Lazarus is dead, though the Lord says he is sleeping (vv. 11–12). In this figurative sense, sleep is found twelve times in addition to the case of Lazarus:

- In martyrdom, Stephen fell asleep (Acts 7:60).

- David fell asleep and was laid beside his ancestors (13:36).

- A woman is free to marry anyone she wishes after her husband falls asleep (1 Corinthians 7:39).

  1. Read 1 Corinthians 11:27–32. What caused some believers in Corinth to be weak and ill and even fall asleep?

  2. In 1 Corinthians 15:17–18, what would be the fate of those who have fallen asleep if Christ had not been raised from the dead?

- Some of those who saw the Lord in resurrection were still alive, though some had fallen asleep (1 Corinthians 15:6).

- Christ is the firstfruits of those who have fallen asleep (v. 20).

- We will not all fall asleep, but we will all be changed (v. 51).

- Paul did not want the believers to grieve in the same way others do over those who had fallen asleep (1 Thessalonians 4:13).

  3. In 1 Thessalonians 4:14, what logically follows our belief that Jesus died and rose again?

- Those who are alive at the time of the Lord's second coming will not meet him before those who are asleep (1 Thessalonians 4:15).

- Doubters say, "Ever since our ancestors fell asleep, all things continue as they were from the beginning of creation" (2 Peter 3:4 NRSV).

By likening death with sleep, the scripture indicates that death has the beneficial aspect of sleep: It restores us to physical vitality. However, death itself is an enemy (1 Corinthians 15:26). So this figure is given its meaning in the pleasant awakening of resurrection.

Day Seventy-Seven

John 11:30–44

30 Now Jesus was not yet come into the town, but was in that place where Martha met him.

31 The Jews then which were with her in the house, and comforted her, when they saw Mary, that she rose up hastily and went out, followed her, saying, She goeth unto the grave to weep there.

32 Then when Mary was come where Jesus was, and saw him, she fell down at his feet, saying unto him, Lord, if thou hadst been here, my brother had not died.

33 When Jesus therefore saw her weeping, and the Jews also weeping which came with her, he groaned in the spirit, and was troubled.

34 And said, Where have ye laid him? They said unto him, Lord, come and see.

35 Jesus wept.

36 Then said the Jews, Behold how he loved him!

37 And some of them said, Could not this man, which opened the eyes of the blind, have caused that even this man should not have died?

38 Jesus therefore again groaning in himself cometh to the grave. It was a cave, and a stone lay upon it.

39 Jesus said, Take ye away the stone. Martha, the sister of him that was dead, saith unto him, Lord, by this time he stinketh: for he hath been dead four days.

40 Jesus saith unto her, Said I not unto thee, that, if thou wouldest believe, thou shouldest see the glory of God?

41 Then they took away the stone from the place where the dead was laid. And Jesus lifted up his eyes, and said, Father, I thank thee that thou hast heard me.

42 And I knew that thou hearest me always: but because of the people which stand by I said it, that they may believe that thou hast sent me.

43 And when he thus had spoken, he cried with a loud voice, Lazarus, come forth.

44 And he that was dead came forth, bound hand and foot with graveclothes: and his face was bound about with a napkin. Jesus saith unto them, Loose him, and let him go.

The Death and Resurrection of Lazarus

Doesn't it seem strange that the Lord says, "Lazarus is dead. And I am glad" (John 11:14–15)? I would have said, "I am sad." Can the light of scripture allow us to look upon death and be glad? Calamities certainly bring no joy, but consider the glory that will be God's when death is dealt with.

1. Read Hebrews 12:2. Why did Christ endure death on the cross?

2. 1 Corinthians 15:22 says that in Adam all people die. According to this verse, which people are made alive in Christ?

"Jesus wept" (John 11:35). Don't his tears reveal tender compassion (Luke 19:41)? Yet he says he is glad that his friend died. Though he has the power to heal Lazarus's sickness, he deliberately stays away. This ensures that Lazarus will die (vv. 5–6). Why would the Lord do this? Because this man's death prepared for the revelation of God's glory in resurrection.

Therefore, Jesus Christ comforts Mary and Martha with the great truth that he is the resurrection and the life (vv. 25–26). But in him, truth is not stern, heartless dogma. It does not override natural feelings or condemn sorrow as unbelief. His heart is moved with compassion. He stops to mingle his tears with theirs. Then he wipes them all away by his marvelous miracle. Similarly, the apostle Paul does not forbid grieving. Instead, he reveals the truth of resurrection so that the believers would not sorrow in the same manner as those who have no such hope (1 Thessalonians 4:13).

3. In 2 Corinthians 6:10, Paul was sorrowful. What accompanied his sorrow?

Christ is glad that Lazarus has died. Still, he has deep feelings for his friends who do not yet share his understanding of resurrection. Grief should stir our emotions. God has designed it to bring us to tears. Otherwise, it fails to accomplish the purpose for which it exists. Its ultimate value is found in contrast with the sheer joy for which it prepares us.

The Lord raised three people from the dead:

- Jairus's daughter had only just died (Mark 5:35–42).

- The son of the widow of Nain was on the way to burial (Luke 7:11–16).

- Lazarus had been dead long enough to be offensive.

"Lord, already there is a stench because he has been dead four days," said Martha (John 11:39 NRSV). Who wants to see a rotting corpse? Yet Christ tells them they will see God's glory (v. 40). How is it possible to open a grave and see the glory of God? Actually, this is the only place on this earth where glory can be fully manifested. The scriptures give many examples that illustrate the valuable function of evil in the universe: It reveals God. If Lazarus had not died, we would not know Christ as the resurrection and life.

Even Mary, who sat at his feet intently listening to Jesus Christ as he taught, had no idea of this (Luke 10:29). He was deeply moved and greatly disturbed in spirit when Mary came to him weeping, "Lord, if you had been here, my brother would not have died" (vv. 32–33). Did she know that he had delayed his arrival?

4. Read Genesis 2:9. Who planted the tree of the knowledge of good and evil in the Garden of Eden?

The resurrection of Lazarus answers these baffling questions: Why does God allow evil? Why does he not come and remove it from the earth? Christ's delay confirms the great truth that both good and evil are from God (Isaiah 45:7). Good cannot be known and appreciated except in the presence of evil. The revelation of resurrection needs Lazarus's loathsome corpse.

Day Seven

He had no form... in his appearance... others hid... (vv. 3...)

John 12:36–43

36 While ye have light, believe in the light... dren of light. These things spake Jesus, and... himself from them.

37 But though he had done so many miracle... believed not on him:

38 That the saying of Esaias the prophet might... which he spake, Lord, who hath believed our report? and ...hom hath the arm of the Lord been revealed?

39 Therefore they could not believe, because that Esaias said again,

40 He hath blinded their eyes, and hardened their heart; that they should not see with their eyes, nor understand with their heart, and be converted, and I should heal them.

41 These things said Esaias, when he saw his glory, and spake of him.

42 Nevertheless among the chief rulers also many believed on him; but because of the Pharisees they did not confess him, lest they should be put out of the synagogue:

43 For they loved the praise of men more than the praise of God.

The End of Christ's Public Ministry

"While you have the light," said Jesus, "believe in the light" (John 12:36 NRSV). But instead of becoming children of light, the crowd continued to walk in darkness, rejecting the Son of Man just as the prophet Isaiah foretold (v. 38; Isaiah 53:1).

1. According to John 3:19, why do people love darkness instead of light?

At this point, Jesus Christ's public ministry ends. So John asks Isaiah's question: "Who has believed what we have heard? And to whom has the arm of the Lord been revealed?" (53:1 NRSV). The answer: By that time, nearly no one has seen or believed. Therefore, as if to fulfill the prophet's words, Christ hides himself:

or majesty that we should look at him, nothing
that we should desire him. . .and as one from whom
their faces; he was despised, and we held him of no account
4).

In each of the four accounts of Christ's life, this juncture is marked by the quote from Isaiah 6:9–10 (John 12:40; see also Matthew 13:14, Mark 4:12, and Luke 8:10). This message of Israel's doom is always quoted when their apostasy is beyond repair. It separates the Lord's ministry into two distinct periods.

• First, Jesus Christ speaks to Israel about the kingdom. This continues until its rejection.

• Then he speaks to his closest followers about his suffering and death. This continues until he is betrayed.

This pattern is repeated with the apostles' ministry in the book of Acts. There, the kingdom is again proclaimed to the whole nation of Israel. When their rejection is final, Paul quotes Isaiah 6:9–10 and Israel is set aside until the full number of the Gentiles has come in (Acts 28:25–28; Romans 11:25–26). The rejection of the Messiah by God's chosen people opened the door for our present enjoyment of transcendent grace.

2. Read John 12:40. Who blinded the eyes of the Jews to Jesus Christ?

3. According to Ephesians 3:8, where do we get the faith to believe in Jesus Christ?

Christians often speak of human responsibility—that is: Those who reject the light deserve the judgment they have invited. But let us pause and consider what has occurred according to John 12. These people had heard the most powerful of all preachers and seen the most marvelous of all miracle workers (v. 37), yet we are clearly told that they could not believe.

4. In John 12:38, what is the reason for the people's unbelief?

The scriptures reveal that God's purpose requires a measure of both unbelief and faith. Romans 11:32 confirms this: "For God has bound all men over to disobedience so that he may have mercy on them all" (NIV).

Day Seventy-Nine

John 13:16–30

16 Verily, verily, I say unto you, The servant is not greater than his lord; neither he that is sent greater than he that sent him.

17 If ye know these things, happy are ye if ye do them.

18 I speak not of you all: I know whom I have chosen: but that the scripture may be fulfilled, He that eateth bread with me hath lifted up his heel against me.

19 Now I tell you before it come, that, when it is come to pass, ye may believe that I am he.

20 Verily, verily, I say unto you, He that receiveth whomsoever I send receiveth me; and he that receiveth me receiveth him that sent me.

21 When Jesus had thus said, he was troubled in spirit, and testified, and said, Verily, verily, I say unto you, that one of you shall betray me.

22 Then the disciples looked one on another, doubting of whom he spake.

23 Now there was leaning on Jesus' bosom one of his disciples, whom Jesus loved.

24 Simon Peter therefore beckoned to him, that he should ask who it should be of whom he spake.

25 He then lying on Jesus' breast saith unto him, Lord, who is it?

26 Jesus answered, He it is, to whom I shall give a sop, when I have dipped it. And when he had dipped the sop, he gave it to Judas Iscariot, the son of Simon.

27 And after the sop Satan entered into him. Then said Jesus unto him, That thou doest, do quickly.

28 Now no man at the table knew for what intent he spake this unto him.

29 For some of them thought, because Judas had the bag, that Jesus had said unto him, Buy those things that we have need of against the feast; or, that he should give something to the poor.

30 He then having received the sop went immediately out: and it was night.

Jesus Feeds Judas

The Lord actually chose Judas to be one of his disciples (Matthew 10:4). He knew him well and even quoted the prophecy that foretells his treachery and betrayal (John 13:18; Psalm 41:9). Why did Christ allow such a man within his circle of trusted friends? He chose Judas for one purpose: Betrayal.

1. Read John 6:70–71. What did Jesus call Judas?

However, Christ never betrayed Judas to the other disciples. This is marvelous. He treated him just as he did the others. Judas's true character was concealed from them so well that they did not guess why he went out from the supper (John 13:27–29) or understand what the Lord said concerning him (v. 26). His treatment of Judas is worth copying.

2. In John 13:26, what is the method the Lord used to indicate his betrayer?

In those days, all eating was done with the fingers. A small piece of thin, hard biscuit was used to pass food from bowl to mouth. This was eaten like we eat a chip with dip. Again, John uses images of food to reveal the character and commission of Jesus Christ.

Consider the way Christ points out his betrayer: How kind and delicate it is to feed another, like a mother her child. Giving a guest a morsel in this way was the highest mark of respect and honor from a host to his guest. No wonder not one of the disciples, except John, the writer of this account, knew what it meant. It was the last loving act of the Lord for Judas. Only the betrayer could understand its meaning. The others would look upon it as a special mark of favor.

3. Read Luke 22:47–48. What was the signal Judas used when betraying his master?

Whirling about the peaceful scene in the upper room are invisible powers of darkness. Judas is not capable of committing capital crime on his own. After all, he is only a petty thief (John 12:4–6). So, Satan personally enters him, forcing him forward, controlling his mind and his actions until its accomplishment (13:27). Judas is not himself when he betrays the Messiah.

Later he realizes what he has done, his heart is filled with bitter regret, and he throws the blood money into the faces of the chief priests, acknowledging his terrible trespass (Matthew 27:3–5; Zechariah 11:12–13). The chief priests, however, share none of Judas's remorse. They carefully gather the thirty pieces of silver from off the temple floor and, though involved in the very act of murdering their Messiah, are concerned with a minute point of law (v. 6).

4. Read Matthew 27:1–3. What did the chief priests do that caused Judas to repent? (See verse 1.)

DAY EIGHTY

John 14:9–18

9 Jesus saith unto him, Have I been so long time with you, and yet hast thou not known me, Philip? he that hath seen me hath seen the Father; and how sayest thou then, Show us the Father?

10 Believest thou not that I am in the Father, and the Father in me? the words that I speak unto you I speak not of myself: but the Father that dwelleth in me, he doeth the works.

11 Believe me that I am in the Father, and the Father in me: or else believe me for the very works' sake.

12 Verily, verily, I say unto you, He that believeth on me, the works that I do shall he do also; and greater works than these shall he do; because I go unto my Father.

13 And whatsoever ye shall ask in my name, that will I do, that the Father may be glorified in the Son.

14 If ye shall ask any thing in my name, I will do it.

15 If ye love me, keep my commandments.

16 And I will pray the Father, and he shall give you another Comforter, that he may abide with you for ever;

17 Even the Spirit of truth; whom the world cannot receive, because it seeth him not, neither knoweth him: but ye know him; for he dwelleth with you, and shall be in you.

18 I will not leave you comfortless: I will come to you.

The Coming of the Spirit

Now, the cold shadow of the cross falls upon the Lord's soul. Yet he is concerned for the sorrows of the disciples. He is about to leave them through humiliation and cruel death. Then, they will need solace and relief.

1. Read John 7:37–39. How is the Spirit described in these verses? (See verse 38.)

Sorrow is about to engulf his beloved friends. This is why Jesus Christ calls the Spirit a comforter. Later it will break forth within them like a river, but its first task will be to console them after the death of their master.

The Lord calls it the Spirit of truth because God's saints find comfort in the truth (John 14:17). The world cannot receive this Spirit. Instead, it seeks relief in the false philosophy of the spirit of deception (1 John 4:6). This spirit is sweeping the world forward to the end of this age and the worship of the antichrist (Revelation 13:8).

2. In John 6:63, what is the function of the Spirit?

When Adam was formed from the soil, God breathed life into him. The man became a living soul (Genesis 2:7). This event corresponds with Christ's action in John 20:22 where he breathed into the disciples and said, "Receive the Holy Spirit." In the garden, God's breath made Adam a living soul. In the locked room, Christ's breath gave the disciples spiritual life.

3. Read 1 Corinthians 15:45. In this verse, what is Adam?
   What is Christ (the last Adam)?

When the twelve apostles set forth on their ministry to Israel, repentance and baptism were required for receipt of the Spirit (Acts 2:38). When the gospel was first taken beyond Jerusalem, it was given when believers associated with the apostles (8:15–17). In our day, without human intermediaries, the Spirit is the portion of all who simply believe (Ephesians 1:13).

DAY EIGHTY-ONE

John 15:1–5

1 I am the true vine, and my Father is the husbandman.

2 Every branch in me that beareth not fruit he taketh away: and every branch that beareth fruit, he purgeth it, that it may bring forth more fruit.

3 Now ye are clean through the word which I have spoken unto you.

4 Abide in me, and I in you. As the branch cannot bear fruit of itself, except it abide in the vine; no more can ye, except ye abide in me.

5 I am the vine, ye are the branches: He that abideth in me, and I in him, the same bringeth forth much fruit: for without me ye can do nothing.

The Vine and the Body

The fig, the olive, and the vine are used by God to picture the political, the spiritual, and social blessedness of Israel as a nation. In Judges 9:10 the fig tree is asked to be a king. Romans chapter 11 tells of the spiritual flow in an olive tree (v. 17). Psalm 80 shows Israel as a vine brought out of Egypt, and planted deep in the Promised Land. Though it filled the land, God destroyed it (vv. 8–16).

1. According to Isaiah 5:7, to what does the prophet liken the vineyard of the Lord?

Jeremiah sees Israel as an excellent, cultivated vine. But it degenerates and turns wild (2:21). In the parable of the trees, the vine declares that its wine gladdens both God and mortals (Judges 9:13). But later, Hosea cries:

Israel is a luxuriant vine that yields its fruit. The more his fruit increased the more altars he built; as his country improved, he improved his pillars (10:1 NRSV).

Here in John, Jesus Christ informs his disciples that he is the true vine (John 15:1). The fruitless branches mentioned by Israel's prophets have been removed (v. 2). But the disciples are cleansed by the belief in the truth, abide in him, and bear fruit (vv. 3–5). However, one verse later, this lovely pastoral image turns serious:

> *If anyone does not remain in me, he is like a branch that is thrown away and withers; such branches are picked up, thrown into the fire, and burned (v. 6 NIV).*

The salvation proclaimed to Israel by Jesus Christ and the twelve apostles was conditional. To avoid the fire, a branch must remain in the vine by its own effort. This idea is found in the book of Hebrews, which was written to those Jews who believed through the ministry of the Twelve. If they did not pay attention to what they had heard, they could drift away (2:1). They remained God's house if they held fast to the confidence of their hope (3:6). They could actually withdraw from the living God (3:12). Tragically, many of those who were enlightened through the apostles ministry in Jerusalem fell away (6:4–6). These did not abide in the vine. They withered and burned.

2. In John 15:10, what is the condition for abiding in the Lord's love?

Although the understanding of Christ as the vine can teach us valuable spiritual lessons, strictly speaking, we are not branches in the vine. Rather, we are blessed to be members of the body of Christ (Ephesians 5:30). Members of a body cannot be lopped off like the branches of a vine. We are saved by pure grace and do not depend on our own abiding, but on God's power and love. The gospel of grace is not conditional; it does not depend upon our ability to do anything (Ephesians 2:8–9). We are vitally a part of Christ himself. He would be maimed if members of his body were cut out.

3. 1 Timothy says that we are called with a holy calling. What is the basis of our calling?

4. Titus 3:5 says that we were not saved by our works of righteousness. According to this verse, what is the basis of God's salvation?

Day Eighty-Two

John 15:12–19

12 This is my commandment, That ye love one another, as I have loved you.

13 Greater love hath no man than this, that a man lay down his life for his friends.

14 Ye are my friends, if ye do whatsoever I command you.

15 Henceforth I call you not servants; for the servant knoweth not what his lord doeth: but I have called you friends; for all things that I have heard of my Father I have made known unto you.

16 Ye have not chosen me, but I have chosen you, and ordained you, that ye should go and bring forth fruit, and that your fruit should remain: that whatsoever ye shall ask of the Father in my name, he may give it you.

17 These things I command you, that ye love one another.

18 If the world hate you, ye know that it hated me before it hated you.

19 If ye were of the world, the world would love his own: but because ye are not of the world, but I have chosen you out of the world, therefore the world hateth you.

The Love of God in Christ Jesus

As he proclaimed the kingdom gospel, the Lord explained that the whole law is included in the word *love* (Matthew 22:37–40). The entire Jewish law and prophets hinge on these two commands: Love God and love mankind. Now, in the midst of his final instructions to his disciples the Lord gives the greatest example of love the universe has seen or ever will see (John 15:13). They will soon witness him offering his soul to God for the sin of the world. Then their hearts will be fully persuaded of love's excellent way (1 Corinthians 12:31).

1. Today, God's economy is described in three words: faith, hope and love. In 1 Corinthians 13:13, what is the greatest of these?

Paul, the apostle to the Gentiles, always stresses love. Our salvation is not based on law or precepts (Colossians 2:13–14). Our life in love needs no law; it soars far above all the law's righteous demands. So the apostle wrote, "The one who loves another has fulfilled the law" (Romans 13:8 NRSV).

2. Romans 13:9–10 gives a definition of love. What is this?
(See verse 10.)

Salvation reveals God's love. All active effort in our salvation comes from God. It is the outflow of divine love. However, salvation is often considered a matter of choice even though the scripture says, "There is no one who seeks God" (Romans 3:11 NRSV).

Paul himself is the chief example of God's loving salvation in pure grace. He describes himself as a former blasphemer, a persecutor, and a man of violence—the foremost of sinners. But the Lord's grace overflows to him in grace and love in Christ Jesus (1 Timothy 1:13–16).

Paul did his utmost to destroy the church. He approved of Stephen's murder and went from house to house arresting the believers. (For accounts of his experience, read Acts 9 and 22.) Picture Paul traveling the road to Damascus to arrest believers there and bring them to Jerusalem for punishment. He is a murderer in active opposition to God's will; as far from God as he can be with no thought of becoming a Christian.

3. Read Acts 9:13. What was Ananias's opinion of Paul?

Paul is the perfect example of God's love because he did absolutely nothing to find salvation. "Suddenly a light from heaven flashed around him [and] he asked, "Who are you Lord?" (Acts 9:3–5 NRSV). This begins the career of the man chosen to bring God's name to the Gentiles, to kings, and the people of Israel (v. 15); the man who wrote half of the New Testament.

But divine love is most powerfully seen in God's calling of the nations. "For he chose us in him before the creation of the world to be holy and blameless in his sight. In love, he predestined us to be adopted as his sons through Jesus Christ, in accordance with his pleasure and will" (Ephesians 1:4–5 NIV).

In Christ, God chose us before the foundation of the world. Sin came into the world *after* we were chosen. In other words, sin cannot affect God's graceful purpose for us. God chooses us and calls us. Ultimately, God glorifies us (Romans 8:29–30). In other words, God loves us.

4. Read Romans 8:35–39. What can separate us from the love of God?

DAY EIGHTY-THREE

John 16:7–16

7 Nevertheless I tell you the truth; It is expedient for you that I go away: for if I go not away, the Comforter will not come unto you; but if I depart, I will send him unto you.

8 And when he is come, he will reprove the world of sin, and of righteousness, and of judgment:

9 Of sin, because they believe not on me;

10 Of righteousness, because I go to my Father, and ye see me no more;

11 Of judgment, because the prince of this world is judged.

12 I have yet many things to say unto you, but ye cannot bear them now.

13 Howbeit when he, the Spirit of truth, is come, he will guide you into all truth: for he shall not speak of himself; but whatsoever he shall hear, that shall he speak: and he will shew you things to come.

14 He shall glorify me: for he shall receive of mine, and shall shew it unto you.

15 All things that the Father hath are mine: therefore said I, that he shall take of mine, and shall shew it unto you.

16 A little while, and ye shall not see me: and again, a little while, and ye shall see me, because I go to the Father.

The Ministry of the Spirit

How surprising to hear the Lord say, "I still have many things to say to you, but you cannot bear them now" (John 16:12 NRSV). This means the Lord's words in the four gospels do not tell us all he had to say. This is because his hearers were limited. Christ's closest disciples could not understand some of the simplest facts.

1. In Matthew 16:21, the Lord tells the disciples of his suffering, death, and resurrection. In verse 22, what is Peter's response to this information?

The Lord even assumed they understood things that were still a puzzle to them. He told them of his departure: "You know the way to the place where I am going" (John 14:4 NRSV). But Thomas said, "Lord, we do not know where you are going. How can we know the way?" (v. 5). A universe of truth was awaiting revelation in Christ's death, resurrection, and exaltation. The disciples could not begin to understand these things.

2. Read John 15:26. What is the function of the Spirit of truth?

After Jesus Christ is silenced by death, the transcendent truths of scripture are given through the Spirit of truth. "He will guide you into all truth. . .he will show you things to come" (John 16:13). The Spirit is given a much larger place in the writings of Paul than elsewhere in scripture. There we are led into all truth and see the things to come.

3. Read 2 Corinthians 3:3. With what was Paul's ministry written? Where is it written?

The Spirit of truth enabled Paul to "complete the word of God" (Colossians 1:25). By the Spirit, he takes us back before Genesis chapter 1 (Ephesians 1:4), and brings us forward past Revelation chapter 22 (1 Corinthians 15:24–26, 28). No wonder he described his ministry of the Spirit as "even more glorious" (2 Corinthians 3:8).

DAY EIGHTY-FOUR

John 17:18–26

18 As thou hast sent me into the world, even so have I also sent them into the world.

19 And for their sakes I sanctify myself, that they also might be sanctified through the truth.

20 Neither pray I for these alone, but for them also which shall believe on me through their word;

21 That they all may be one; as thou, Father, art in me, and I in thee, that they also may be one in us: that the world may believe that thou hast sent me.

22 And the glory which thou gavest me I have given them; that they may be one, even as we are one:

23 I in them, and thou in me, that they may be made perfect in one; and that the world may know that thou hast sent me, and hast loved them, as thou hast loved me.

24 Father, I will that they also, whom thou hast given me, be with me where I am; that they may behold my glory, which thou hast given me: for thou lovedst me before the foundation of the world.

25 O righteous Father, the world hath not known thee: but I have known thee, and these have known that thou hast sent me.

26 And I have declared unto them thy name, and will declare it: that the love wherewith thou hast loved me may be in them, and I in them.

The Father's Gift to the Son

The disciples were a gift from the Father to the Son (John 17:24). Jesus Christ valued them, not only for their own sakes, but also because of the giver. Here, human lives are interwoven into the love between God and Christ. This thought gives cause for great comfort. That is, our lives are bound up with the love of God for the Son. They are the topic of the Son's prayerful response to his Father.

1. Read John 17:10. Since we belong to Christ, whose are we? If we are God's, who possesses us?

2. John 6:37–39 also speaks of God's gift to the Son. According to verse 39, what is the destiny of this gift?

In the record of John chapter 6, people murmur and misunderstand Christ. Finally, many of his disciples desert him (v. 66). But this doesn't seem to matter to the Lord. He tells them, "Only God chooses those who come to me." As we might choose a gift for a loved one, so the believers are a gift from the Father to the Son. It is no wonder some people thirst desperately for the Lord (Psalm 42:1). As God's gift, they will no doubt find him. When they do, he receives them as precious presents from his Father. Christ prizes these human gifts because of the giver—his Father. So he will not lose even one of his believers. "I give them eternal life, and they shall never perish; no one can snatch them out of my hand. My Father, who has given them to me, is greater than all; no one can snatch them out of my Father's hand" (John 10:28–29 NIV).

3. In John 17:2, what does Christ give to those God has given him?

DAY EIGHTY-FIVE

John 18:1–11

1 When Jesus had spoken these words, he went forth with his disciples over the brook Cedron, where was a garden, into the which he entered, and his disciples.

2 And Judas also, which betrayed him, knew the place: for Jesus ofttimes resorted thither with his disciples.

3 Judas then, having received a band of men and officers from the chief priests and Pharisees, cometh thither with lanterns and torches and weapons.

4 Jesus therefore, knowing all things that should come upon him, went forth, and said unto them, Whom seek ye?

5 They answered him, Jesus of Nazareth. Jesus saith unto them, I am he. And Judas also, which betrayed him, stood with them.

6 As soon then as he had said unto them, I am he, they went backward, and fell to the ground.

7 Then asked he them again, Whom seek ye? And they said, Jesus of Nazareth.

8 Jesus answered, I have told you that I am he: if therefore ye seek me, let these go their way:

9 That the saying might be fulfilled, which he spake, Of them which thou gavest me have I lost none.

10 Then Simon Peter having a sword drew it, and smote the high priest's servant, and cut off his right ear. The servant's name was Malchus.

11 Then said Jesus unto Peter, Put up thy sword into the sheath: the cup which my Father hath given me, shall I not drink it?

The Prince of Light Meets the Prince of Darkness

It is understandable that the betrayer comes to the garden with lanterns and torches (John 18:3). Night has fallen; Satan fears the light of day when the Lord's work is done (John 12:35). But why does Judas need a squad of soldiers and armed police to arrest a gentle, unarmed man and his timid disciples? In Matthew's account, Jesus wonders the same thing, "Am I leading a rebellion, that you have come out with swords and clubs to capture me? Every day I sat in the temple courts teaching, and you did not arrest me" (Matthew 26:55 NIV).

1. Read Luke 22:52–53. Why did they come to arrest Jesus armed and at night? (See verse 53.)

Despite the show of force, Jesus Christ is in authority even over his own arrest:

- His simple words knock his enemies to the ground (John 18:5).

- He calmly orders them to leave his disciples alone (v. 8).

- He rebukes his disciple's use of force (v. 11).

- In the midst of violence, he heals (Luke 22:50–51).

2. The Lord's arrest begins the fulfillment of the scripture's earliest prophecy in Genesis 3:15. According to this verse, what does Christ do to Satan? What does Satan do to Christ?

Behind the scenes, there is real darkness. These soldiers, police, and conspirators are all under the command of Satan. He had deluded Eve in the Garden of Eden. True to prophecy, he is now hurting the heel of her seed (Genesis 3:15).

3. According to John 8:44, where are these people from?

Here in the garden, Satan has enlisted mankind against Christ. They are clearly children of their father, the devil. Yet, Satan has actually entered into Judas (John 13:27). In him, God's adversary is personally present in this pivotal scene. The prince of light and the prince of darkness here meet in Judas's kiss.

Day Eighty-Six

John 19:17–24

17 And he bearing his cross went forth into a place called the place of a skull, which is called in the Hebrew Golgotha:

18 Where they crucified him, and two other with him, on either side one, and Jesus in the midst.

19 And Pilate wrote a title, and put it on the cross. And the writing was JESUS OF NAZARETH THE KING OF THE JEWS.

20 This title then read many of the Jews: for the place where Jesus was crucified was nigh to the city: and it was written in Hebrew, and Greek, and Latin.

21 Then said the chief priests of the Jews to Pilate, Write not, The King of the Jews; but that he said, I am King of the Jews.

22 Pilate answered, What I have written I have written.

23 Then the soldiers, when they had crucified Jesus, took his garments, and made four parts, to every soldier a part; and also his coat: now the coat was without seam, woven from the top throughout.

24 They said therefore among themselves, Let us not rend it, but cast lots for it, whose it shall be: that the scripture might be fulfilled, which saith, They parted my raiment among them, and for my vesture they did cast lots. These things therefore the soldiers did.

The Curse of the Cross

Moses prescribed stoning as Israel's mode for the death penalty (Leviticus 24:14). It was a comparatively swift and painless death. A single blow on the head would stun the victim into unconsciousness. But the Roman way was far more painful and shameful. They attached their victim's arms above his head to a single upright stake and left him to die. In this position, the weight of the body restricts the ability to breathe. Death comes by slow suffocation—a lingering and humiliating spectacle.

1. Read Galatians 3:13. What did Christ become when he hung on the cross?

There is no glamour in the cross of Christ; no light, only dense darkness; no power, only weakness; no glory, only shame. Christ was lifted up only high enough so his feet did not touch the ground. The shamefulness of crucifixion is the climax to Christ's descent from the highest glory to the lowest humiliation.

2. Philippians 2:6–7 describes Christ's descent. In each verse, he took one main action. What are these?

Christ had once been far above all. In his death, he came down to the lowest depths of degradation. Scripture leaves nothing to the imagination when describing this: "For our sake [God] made him to be sin who knew no sin" (2 Corinthians 5:21).

3. 2 Corinthians 5:21 describes Christ becoming sin for us. According to this verse, what do we become as a result?

The psalmist's song tells a little of what the Lord felt as he hung there:

> I am poured out like water,
> and all my bones are out of joint.
> My heart has turned to wax;
> it has melted away within me.
> My strength is dried up like a potsherd,
> and my tongue sticks to the roof of my mouth;
> you lay me in the dust of death (Psalm 22:14–15 NIV).

Jesus Christ dies at the hands of God, not His enemies. But before this can occur, one more passage of scripture must be satisfied. The Psalmist predicted: "They gave me poison for food, and for my thirst they gave me vinegar" (69:21 NRSV). So he prompts them, "I am thirsty" (John 19:28). Then they fill a sponge with sour wine, lift it to his lips, and fulfill the scripture (v. 29).

4. Read Luke 24:44. What concerning Christ must be fulfilled?

"It is finished" (John 19:30). Jesus Christ accomplished the Father's work. He need not suffer further. So he laid down his soul by his own decision. Christ's death came not because of exhaustion. It was a deliberate act of his will. He bowed his head and gave up his spirit to God.

Day Eighty-Seven

John 20:1–16

1 The first day of the week cometh Mary Magdalene early, when it was yet dark, unto the sepulchre, and seeth the stone taken away from the sepulchre.

2 Then she runneth, and cometh to Simon Peter, and to the other disciple, whom Jesus loved, and saith unto them, They have taken away the Lord out of the sepulchre, and we know not where they have laid him.

3 Peter therefore went forth, and that other disciple, and came to the sepulchre. . . .

7 And the napkin, that was about his head, not lying with the linen clothes, but wrapped together in a place by itself.

8 Then went in also that other disciple, which came first to the sepulchre, and he saw, and believed.

9 For as yet they knew not the scripture, that he must rise again from the dead.

10 Then the disciples went away again unto their own home.

11 But Mary stood without at the sepulchre weeping: and as she wept, she stooped down, and looked into the sepulchre,

12 And seeth two angels in white sitting, the one at the head, and the other at the feet, where the body of Jesus had lain.

13 And they say unto her, Woman, why weepest thou? She saith unto them, Because they have taken away my Lord, and I know not where they have laid him.

14 And when she had thus said, she turned herself back, and saw Jesus standing, and knew not that it was Jesus.

15 Jesus saith unto her, Woman, why weepest thou? whom seekest thou? She, supposing him to be the gardener, saith unto him, Sir, if thou have borne him hence, tell me where thou hast laid him, and I will take him away.

16 Jesus saith unto her, Mary. She turned herself, and saith unto him, Rabboni; which is to say, Master.

Mary Witnesses Christ's Resurrection

Not long before Jesus Christ died, his friend Lazarus had died. Lazarus, however, saw corruption. Christ did not. Lazarus was raised from his grave bound with grave clothes, his face covered with a cloth (John 11:44). These are signs of mortality, the symbols of weakness. But our Lord was raised in power. His feet were free; his hands unbound; his face uncovered. He had folded his grave clothes neatly in his tomb (John 20:6–7).

1. In John 10:17, why does the Lord lay down his life?

Christ had the strength to remove his grave clothes and roll aside the stone. That is, to take up his life again. This shows that he is not merely the resurrection, he is the life (John 11:25).

The first witness to the resurrection is Mary Magdalene. This woman from the town of Magdala had been possessed with seven demons (Mark 16:9). The Lord healed her, and she is listed among the women who materially provided for the Lord and his disciples (Luke 8:2–3). She must have witnessed Joseph of Arimathea and Nicodemus as they laid the Lord in the tomb (John 19:38–42). She and some of the other women are there very early on the morning after the Sabbath to complete the preparation of the Lord's body for burial (20:1; Mark 16:1; Luke 23:55–24:1).

2. Read John 20:1–10. What did Peter and John not know when they viewed the empty tomb?

Unlike Peter and John, Mary does not take a quick look in the tomb and leave. She lingers there weeping (John 20:11), and her faith is rewarded by the indescribable benefit of being first to see the risen Christ. Peter and John only saw the grave clothes (vv. 5–7).

3. Read John 20:12. When Mary Magdalene looked into the tomb, what did she see?

I might have been pleased to see the angels in Christ's tomb. Not so with Mary. She is not satisfied with anyone but her Lord. At first, she only hears his voice speak her name: "Mary" (John 20:16). Immediately she recognizes the voice of her beloved teacher and turns to see the resurrected Lord. Only she, of all the disciples, is told of his victorious ascension to the Father (v. 17).

4. What are the distinctions between believers in Galatians 3:23?

Today in certain churches, women are not allowed to teach. But the resurrected Christ makes no such distinctions. On the first day of this era of resurrection, Mary Magdalene is sent by the resurrected one himself to declare to the disciples his ascension to the Father (vv. 17–18).

DAY EIGHTY-EIGHT

John 20:17-28

17 Jesus saith unto her, Touch me not; for I am not yet ascended to my Father: but go to my brethren, and say unto them, I ascend unto my Father, and your Father; and to my God, and your God.

18 Mary Magdalene came and told the disciples that she had seen the Lord, and that he had spoken these things unto her.

19 Then the same day at evening, being the first day of the week, when the doors were shut where the disciples were assembled for fear of the Jews, came Jesus and stood in the midst, and saith unto them, Peace be unto you.

20 And when he had so said, he shewed unto them his hands and his side. Then were the disciples glad, when they saw the Lord. . . .

22 And when he had said this, he breathed on them, and saith unto them, Receive ye the Holy Ghost. . . .

24 But Thomas, one of the twelve, called Didymus, was not with them when Jesus came.

25 The other disciples therefore said unto him, We have seen the LORD. But he said unto them, Except I shall see in his hands the print of the nails, and put my finger into the print of the nails, and thrust my hand into his side, I will not believe.

26 And after eight days again his disciples were within, and Thomas with them: then came Jesus, the doors being shut, and stood in the midst, and said, Peace be unto you.

27 Then saith he to Thomas, Reach hither thy finger, and behold my hands; and reach hither thy hand, and thrust it into my side: and be not faithless, but believing.

28 And Thomas answered and said unto him, My Lord and my God.

The Ascension of Christ

After his resurrection, Christ ascended twice. The first is indicated in John 20:17. He will not allow Mary to touch him because he is the firstfruit of resurrection. Only God should enjoy his freshness. This is seen in the offerings of Israel: "The choicest of the firstfruits of your ground you shall bring into the house of the Lord your God" (Exodus 23:19).

God's harvest of those who have died began with Christ. God's promise is: "As all die in Adam, so all will be made alive in Christ" (1 Corinthians 15:22 NRSV). But there is an order to the resurrection: "Christ the first fruits, then at his coming those who belong to Christ" (v. 23).

1. 1 Corinthians 15:20 mentions Christ's resurrection. What does this verse call him?

The ascension is proof that Christ's conquest on the cross is not confined to earth. It places him at the head of the whole universe. Angels, sovereignties, authorities, and powers in the heavenly places are all subject to him (Colossians 2:15).

2. In Colossians 2:10, over what is Christ the head?

On the evening of the day of resurrection, Christ returns to breathe the Holy Spirit into the disciples (John 20:19–22). The Lord's second ascension, forty days later, is recorded in Acts 1:9. Christ used the interval between the two ascensions to present proof of his resurrection and to instruct the disciples about the kingdom of God (Acts 1:3). This prepared them for their ministry recorded in Acts.

3. Christ's ascension gives promise of his second coming. In Acts 1:11, what is the angel's description of this?

Christ will return in the same manner in which he ascended. In that day, he will come with the clouds of heaven (Acts 1:9; Daniel 7:13; Revelation 1:7), and his feet will stand on the Mount of Olives (Acts 1:12; Zechariah 14:4).

Day Eighty-Nine

John 21:1–13

1 After these things Jesus shewed himself again to the disciples at the sea of Tiberias; and on this wise shewed he himself.

2 There were together Simon Peter, and Thomas called Didymus, and Nathanael of Cana in Galilee, and the sons of Zebedee, and two other of his disciples.

3 Simon Peter saith unto them, I go a fishing. They say unto him, We also go with thee. They went forth, and entered into a ship immediately; and that night they caught nothing.

4 But when the morning was now come, Jesus stood on the shore: but the disciples knew not that it was Jesus.

5 Then Jesus saith unto them, Children, have ye any meat? They answered him, No.

6 And he said unto them, Cast the net on the right side of the ship, and ye shall find. They cast therefore, and now they were not able to draw it for the multitude of fishes.

7 Therefore that disciple whom Jesus loved saith unto Peter, It is the Lord. Now when Simon Peter heard that it was the Lord, he girt his fisher's coat unto him, (for he was naked,) and did cast himself into the sea. . . .

9 As soon then as they were come to land, they saw a fire of coals there, and fish laid thereon, and bread.

10 Jesus saith unto them, Bring of the fish which ye have now caught.

11 Simon Peter went up, and drew the net to land full of great fishes, an hundred and fifty and three: and for all there were so many, yet was not the net broken.

12 Jesus saith unto them, Come and dine. And none of the disciples durst ask him, Who art thou? knowing that it was the Lord.

13 Jesus then cometh, and taketh bread, and giveth them, and fish likewise.

The Labor and Delivery of Israel

Peter had been commissioned to fish for men (Matthew 4:19). But he returns to his old trade and drags his companions with him to fish for fish. They work all night and despite being professionals, net nothing. This is a lesson in obedience in service to God. Self-will brings much labor but no results. Submission to God's will is weighted with blessing.

1. In John 21:6, what is the result of the fishermen doing the Lord's will?

But there seems to be a deeper lesson here. This is a forecast of Peter's ministry. He and the apostles labored to proclaim the kingdom as recorded in the book of Acts. But, in the end, their efforts did not bring Israel into the kingdom. The nation did not repent. Instead, God closed their eyes and ears to the truth and sent the gospel to the Gentiles (Acts 28:26–28).

2. How does Acts 28:27 describe Israel's heart?

But morning will break; the Messiah will come again; the kingdom will again be proclaimed and the results will be miraculous. All Israel will be saved (Romans 11:26)—a repeat of this miraculous catch of fish. But then, the net will enclose the 144,000 as well as an innumerable throng (Revelation 7:4–10).

The apostle John illustrates this in the figure of the woman in labor (John 16:20–22). Jesus Christ tells his disciples of a day when "you will weep and mourn while the world rejoices. You will grieve, but your grief will turn to joy" (v. 20 NIV). This describes the years of persecution during the great tribulation (Matthew 24:21). Their joy comes on the day of the Messiah's return. The persecution of Israel in the last days of this age is likened to a woman giving birth to a child. She "has pain because her time has come; but when her baby is born she forgets the anguish because of her joy that a child is born into the world" (John 16:21 NIV).

3. Revelation 12:1 describes Israel as a woman. In verse 2, what is this woman doing?

In John 16:22, the Messiah foretells his people's grief without God. Then he promises, "I will see you again and you will rejoice, and no one will take away your joy." That blissful day of the coming kingdom is described in the last chapter of Isaiah:

> Before she was in labor
>   she gave birth;
> before her pain came upon her
>   she delivered a son.
> Who has heard of such a thing?
>   Who has seen such things?
> Shall a land be born in one day?
>   Shall a nation be delivered in one moment?
> Yet as soon as Zion was in labor
>   she delivered her children (66:7–9 NRSV).

DAY NINETY

John 21:15–25

15 So when they had dined, Jesus saith to Simon Peter, Simon, son of Jonas, lovest thou me more than these? He saith unto him, Yea, Lord; thou knowest that I love thee. He saith unto him, Feed my lambs.

16 He saith to him again the second time, Simon, son of Jonas, lovest thou me? He saith unto him, Yea, Lord; thou knowest that I love thee. He saith unto him, Feed my sheep.

17 He saith unto him the third time, Simon, son of Jonas, lovest thou me? Peter was grieved because he said unto him the third time, Lovest thou me? And he said unto him, Lord, thou knowest all things; thou knowest that I love thee. Jesus saith unto him, Feed my sheep.

18 Verily, verily, I say unto thee, When thou wast young, thou girdest thyself, and walkedst whither thou wouldest: but when thou shalt be old, thou shalt stretch forth thy hands, and another shall gird thee, and carry thee whither thou wouldest not.

19 This spake he, signifying by what death he should glorify God. And when he had spoken this, he saith unto him, Follow me.

20 Then Peter, turning about, seeth the disciple whom Jesus loved following; which also leaned on his breast at supper, and said, Lord, which is he that betrayeth thee? . . .

24 This is the disciple which testifieth of these things, and wrote these things: and we know that his testimony is true.

25 And there are also many other things which Jesus did, the which, if they should be written every one, I suppose that even the world itself could not contain the books that should be written. Amen.

The Apostle Peter's Commission

This touching exchange between Peter and his master describes the special commission given to Peter. He fulfilled this in writing his epistles. This is also a satisfying conclusion to Peter's story, who was prominent in his imprudent actions yet was the acknowledged leader of the apostles.

He was humiliated when he disowned the Lord (Luke 22:61–62) and doubted his care and provision (John 21:3). This has chastened his spirit, so he no longer boasts of his loyalty.

1. In Matthew 26:35, what does Peter say he will do before he denies the Lord?

Early in the morning on the beach of the Sea of Galilee, Peter knows that he loves his Lord despite all he has done that might contradict this. But he refuses to boast that he loves him more than the other disciples do (John 21:15). His response is best translated, "Lord, you know that I am *fond* of you." In this answer, Peter uses a weaker word than *love* and appeals to the Lord's omniscience. His humility is rewarded: Christ charges him to feed the lambs; those weak in the faith.

The Lord repeats the question (John 21:16). Peter seems determined never to boast again and so refuses to vouch for himself. "*You know. . . ,*" says the apostle, and is given charge of the Lord's flock—"Shepherd my sheep."

2. Read 1 Peter 5:1–3. What does Peter exhort the elders to do? (See verse 2.)

According to the original Greek text, the third time the Lord questions Peter, he, too, uses the word *fond* instead of *love*. It is as if he questions even this fondness. This hurts Peter deeply, but still he refuses even a hint of boasting (v. 17). Certainly, he feels full of love to the Lord but is painfully aware of his dismal failure. So, he again emphasizes that the Lord is all-knowing—"You know everything." He has learned his lesson well. So the Lord commissions him to provide spiritual food to his sheep, the mature believers.

Peter had once boasted that he would lay down his life for the Lord (13:37). This boast led to the Lord's prediction that Peter would disown him (v. 38). Now he assures Peter that he will indeed, some day, fulfill his boast (21:18–19).

3. In 2 Peter 1:14, the apostle seems to be referring to this incident. What does Peter say about this?

DAY NINETY-ONE

John 7:33

Then said Jesus unto them, Yet a little while am I with you, and then I go unto him that sent me.

John 8:42

Jesus said unto them, If God were your Father, ye would love me: for I proceeded forth and came from God; neither came I of myself, but he sent me.

John 13:1

Now before the feast of the passover, when Jesus knew that his hour was come that he should depart out of this world unto the Father, having loved his own which were in the world, he loved them unto the end.

John 13:3

Jesus knowing that the Father had given all things into his hands, and that he was come from God, and went to God.

John 16:27–28

For the Father himself loveth you, because ye have loved me, and have believed that I came out from God. I came forth from the Father, and am come into the world: again, I leave the world, and go to the Father.

John 16:30

Now are we sure that thou knowest all things, and needest not that any man should ask thee: by this we believe that thou camest forth from God.

John 17:8

For I have given unto them the words which thou gavest me; and they have received them, and have known surely that I came out from thee, and they have believed that thou didst send me.

The Journey of the Son of God

The task of religion, in general, is the attempt to prepare people to come to God. The sacred scripture reveals the opposite. God is prepared to come to us. This idea is summarized in this way: "In Christ God was reconciling the world to himself" (2 Corinthians 5:19 NRSV).

1. Read 2 Corinthians 5:19. How does God account for our sins?

John's story of Christ's life first traces his path from God to us. This can be compared with the path of a priest in the tabernacle—Israel's place of worship in the wilderness. "Have them make me a sanctuary," God told Moses, "so that I may dwell among them" (Exodus 25:8). This tabernacle was designed in three sections separated from the people by a wall of curtains. In the Outer Court were the bronze altar of sacrifice and the laver for washing. This court surrounded a second curtained structure that was divided into two rooms. The innermost was called the Most Holy Place or Holy of Holies where God was present and the Ark of the Covenant was found. The outer chamber was the Holy Place. In it were the incense altar, the lampstand, and the shewbread table. The entrance to the Holy of Holies was through the Holy Place.

2. Hebrews 9:24 says the tabernacle was only a copy of the true one. According to this verse, why did Christ enter the heavenly Holy of Holies?

Some translations of John 1:14 say this: "And the Word became flesh and tabernacled among us." Using this figure, we see Christ's career. In the beginning, the Word is with God in the Holy of Holies (John 1:1). Then he is revealed as the light (1:9), reminding us of the lampstand in the Holy Place. At his baptism, he is at the laver in the Outer Court (1:29; Matthew 3:13). As God's Lamb, he is on the bronze altar of sacrifice to take away the sin of the world (John 1:29, 36). In this way, the Son came out from God.

"He came to his own, and his own people did not accept him" (1:11 NRSV). So Christ goes back to God, the order is reversed, and he is revealed in his priesthood. First, he tells of his death (12:24)—the bronze altar. Next, he washes the disciples' feet (13:5)—the laver. He enters deeper into this figurative tabernacle when he eats his last supper (13:1)—the shewbread table. There in the upper room, he tells of the coming of the Holy Spirit (16:13)—the oil that burns in the lampstand. Then he prays at the incense altar (17:1). Finally, he reenters the Holy of Holies, revealing his glory in the Father's presence (17:5). The Son of God came out from God, accomplished the divine purpose (19:30), and then went back to God (13:3).

3. According to Hebrews 9:12, what did the Son obtain
   when he entered the heavenly Holy of Holies?

God's purpose in sending the Son is summarized in this way: "For our sake [God] made him to be sin who knew no sin, so that in him we might become the righteousness of God" (2 Corinthians 5:21 NRSV). Though the Son has returned to the Father, he left behind an ambassador for this world with the ministry of reconciliation. "We entreat you on behalf of Christ," he says, "be reconciled to God" (v. 20).

Answer Key to
Questions in John

Day Question

64. 1. Two doves.
    2. They followed Jesus.
    3. They led him away to the slaughter.

65. 1. Yes.
    2. Yes. (See John 13:11.)
    3. They will turn to other gods.

66. 1. God was their husband.
    2. God divorced Israel.
    3. In the last days (NIV).
    4. A bride adorned for her husband.

67. 1. "Out of the believers heart shall flow rivers of living water."
    2. The Spirit.
    3. Belief in Jesus Christ.

68. 1. One-fourth of the inhabitants of earth are killed.
    2. Voices in heaven proclaim, "The kingdom of the world has become the kingdom of our Lord and of his Messiah" (NRSV).
    3. The leaves of the tree of life.

69. 1. Every word that comes from the mouth of God.
    2. The knowledge of the Lord.
    3. God's grace is made perfect in man's weakness.

70. 1. Because they complained against Moses and Aaron.
    2. The bread that came down from heaven (see John 6:41, 58).
    3. By believing in him.

71. 1. According to the definite plan and foreknowledge of God.
    2. He came from the Father, and he was going to the Father.
    3. Because he had the words of eternal life.

72. 1. The Son reveals the Father.
    2. He was born in human likeness and found in human form.
    3. All things in heaven and on earth.
    4. God is all in all.

73. 1. When sin increases, grace abounds even more.
    2. All are made alive in Christ.
    3. Death.
    4. Death is thrown in the lake of fire.

74. 1. So that "seeing they do not perceive, and hearing they do not listen, nor do they understand" (NRSV).
    2. He was pierced while he was dying on the cross.
    3. He worshiped.
    4. They denied they were blind.

75. 1. As a shepherd, he had killed lions and bears.
    2. The divine shepherd's rod and staff.
    3. Tend the flock of God.
    4. He makes them complete.

76. 1. They partook of the Lord's Table in an unworthy manner.
    2. They would have perished.
    3. God will bring with him those who have died.

77. 1. For the joy that was set before him.
    2. All are made alive in Christ.
    3. Rejoicing.
    4. God.

78. 1. Because their deeds are evil.
    2. God has blinded their eyes and hardened their hearts.
    3. Faith is a gift from God.
    4. So Isaiah's prophecy could be fulfilled.

79. 1. A devil.
    2. The betrayer was the one to whom the Lord gave a piece of bread that he had dipped in the bowl.
    3. A kiss.
    4. They decided to put Jesus to death.

80. 1. The Spirit is like rivers of living waters.
    2. The Spirit gives life.
    3. The first man Adam became a living soul. The last Adam became a life-giving Spirit.

81. 1. The house of Israel.
    2. Keep the Lord's commandments.
    3. "Not according to our works but according to his own purpose and grace" (NRSV).
    4. Salvation is according to God's mercy through the washing of rebirth and renewal of the Holy Spirit.

82. 1. Love.
    2. Love is the fulfilling of the law.
    3. He was an evildoer.
    4. "Neither death, nor life, nor angels, no rulers, nor things present, nor things to come, nor powers, nor height, nor depth, nor anything else in all creation, will be able to separate us from the love of God in Christ Jesus our Lord" (Romans 8:38–39 NRSV).

83. 1. This must never happen to you.
    2. He testifies for Christ.
    3. Paul's ministry is written with the Spirit on tablets of human hearts.

84. 1. Those who are Christ's are God's as well. God's possessions are also Christ's.
    2. Christ will raise them up on the last day.
    3. Eternal life.

85. 1. "This is your hour," said Jesus, "and the power of darkness."
   2. Christ strikes his head. Satan strikes his heel (NRSV).
   3. They are from their father the devil.

86. 1. A curse for us.
   2. He emptied himself (v. 7); he humbled himself (v. 8).
   3. We become the righteousness of God in him.
   4. Everything written in the Law of Moses, the Prophets, and the Psalms.

87. 1. So that he can take it up again.
   2. They did not understand the scripture—that Christ would rise from the dead.
   3. Two angels in white.
   4. There are none. All are one in Christ Jesus.

88. 1. The first fruits of those who have died.
   2. He is the head over every ruler and authority.
   3. He will come back in the same way as the disciples saw him go into heaven.

89. 1. They caught a multitude of fish.
   2. It has grown dull.
   3. She is giving birth.

90. 1. He will die rather than deny the Lord.
   2. Tend the flock of God.
   3. That his death would come soon.

91. 1. God does not count our sins against us.
   2. To appear for us in God's presence.
   3. Eternal redemption.

About the Author

DANIEL PARTNER, a veteran Christian author and editor, lives in Coos Bay, Oregon. His books include *I Give Myself to Prayer, All Things Are Possible, Peace Like a River, Women of Sacred Song* (written with his wife, Margaret), and *The One-Year Book of Poetry* (coedited with Philip Comfort). All are available at Christian bookstores nationwide.

Besides his publishing work, Daniel is active in preserving and performing mid-nineteenth-century American popular music. Contact him by e-mail at author@danpartner.com.

BIBLE READINGS FOR JANUARY

January 1 - LUKE 5:27–39, GENESIS 1–2, PSALM 1
January 2 - LUKE 6:1–26, GENESIS 3–5, PSALM 2
January 3 - LUKE 6:27–49, GENESIS 6–7, PSALM 3
January 4 - LUKE 7:1–17, GENESIS 8–10, PSALM 4
January 5 - LUKE 7:18–50, GENESIS 11, PSALM 5
January 6 - LUKE 8:1–25, GENESIS 12, PSALM 6
January 7 - LUKE 8:26–56, GENESIS 13–14, PSALM 7
January 8 - LUKE 9:1–27, GENESIS 15, PSALM 8
January 9 - LUKE 9:28–62, GENESIS 16, PSALM 9
January 10 - LUKE 10:1–20, GENESIS 17, PSALM 10
January 11 - LUKE 10:21–42, GENESIS 18, PSALM 11
January 12 - LUKE 11:1–28, GENESIS 19, PSALM 12
January 13 - LUKE 11:29–54, GENESIS 20, PSALM 13
January 14 - LUKE 12:1–31, GENESIS 21, PSALM 14
January 15 - LUKE 12:32–59, GENESIS 22, PSALM 15
January 16 - LUKE 13:1–17, GENESIS 23, PSALM 16
January 17 - LUKE 13:18–35, GENESIS 24, PSALM 17
January 18 - LUKE 14:1–24, GENESIS 25, PSALM 18
January 19 - LUKE 14:25–35, GENESIS 26, PSALM 19
January 20 - LUKE 15, GENESIS 27:1–45, PSALM 20
January 21 - LUKE 16, GENESIS 27:46–28:22, PSALM 21
January 22 - LUKE 17, GENESIS 29:1–30, PSALM 22
January 23 - LUKE 18:1–17, GENESIS 29:31–30:43, PSALM 23
January 24 - LUKE 18:18–43, GENESIS 31, PSALM 24
January 25 - LUKE 19:1–27, GENESIS 32–33, PSALM 25
January 26 - LUKE 19:28–48, GENESIS 34, PSALM 26
January 27 - LUKE 20:1–26, GENESIS 35–36, PSALM 27
January 28 - LUKE 20:27–47, GENESIS 37, PSALM 28
January 29 - LUKE 21, GENESIS 38, PSALM 29
January 30 - LUKE 22:1–38, GENESIS 39, PSALM 30
January 31 - LUKE 22:39–71, GENESIS 40, PSALM 31

Bible Readings for February

February 1 - LUKE 23:1–25, GENESIS 41, PSALM 32
February 2 - LUKE 23:26–56, GENESIS 42, PSALM 33
February 3 - LUKE 24:1–12, GENESIS 43, PSALM 34
February 4 - LUKE 24:13–53, GENESIS 44, PSALM 35
February 5 - HEBREWS 1, GENESIS 45:1–46:27, PSALM 36
February 6 - HEBREWS 2, GENESIS 46:28–47:31, PSALM 37
February 7 - HEBREWS 3:1–4:13, GENESIS 48, PSALM 38
February 8 - HEBREWS 4:14–6:12, GENESIS 49–50, PSALM 39
February 9 - HEBREWS 6:13–20, EXODUS 1–2, PSALM 40
February 10 - HEBREWS 7, EXODUS 3–4, PSALM 41
February 11 - HEBREWS 8, EXODUS 5:1–6:27, PROVERBS 1
February 12 - HEBREWS 9:1–22, EXODUS 6:28–8:32, PROVERBS 2
February 13 - HEBREWS 9:23–10:18, EXODUS 9–10, PROVERBS 3
February 14 - HEBREWS 10:19–39, EXODUS 11–12, PROVERBS 4
February 15 - HEBREWS 11:1–22, EXODUS 13–14, PROVERBS 5
February 16 - HEBREWS 11:23–40, EXODUS 15, PROVERBS 6:1–7:5
February 17 - HEBREWS 12, EXODUS 16–17, PROVERBS 7:6–27
February 18 - HEBREWS 13, EXODUS 18–19, PROVERBS 8
February 19 - MATTHEW 1, EXODUS 20–21, PROVERBS 9
February 20 - MATTHEW 2, EXODUS 22–23, PROVERBS 10
February 21 - MATTHEW 3, EXODUS 24, PROVERBS 11
February 22 - MATTHEW 4, EXODUS 25–27, PROVERBS 12
February 23 - MATTHEW 5:1–20, EXODUS 28–29, PROVERBS 13
February 24 - MATTHEW 5:21–48, EXODUS 30–32, PROVERBS 14
February 25 - MATTHEW 6:1–18, EXODUS 33–34, PROVERBS 15
February 26 - MATTHEW 6:19–34, EXODUS 35–36, PROVERBS 16
February 27 - MATTHEW 7, EXODUS 37–38, PROVERBS 17
February 28 - MATTHEW 8:1–13, EXODUS 39–40, PROVERBS 18

Bible Readings for March

March 1 - Matthew 8:14–34, Leviticus 1–2, Proverbs 19
March 2 - Matthew 9:1–17, Leviticus 3–4, Proverbs 20
March 3 - Matthew 9:18–38, Leviticus 5–6, Proverbs 21
March 4 - Matthew 10:1–25, Leviticus 7–8, Proverbs 22
March 5 - Matthew 10:26–42, Leviticus 9–10, Proverbs 23
March 6 - Matthew 11:1–19, Leviticus 11–12, Proverbs 24
March 7 - Matthew 11:20–30, Leviticus 13, Proverbs 25
March 8 - Matthew 12:1–21, Leviticus 14, Proverbs 26
March 9 - Matthew 12:22–50, Leviticus 15–16, Proverbs 27
March 10 - Matthew 13:1–23, Leviticus 17–18, Proverbs 28
March 11 - Matthew 13:24–58, Leviticus 19, Proverbs 29
March 12 - Matthew 14:1–21, Leviticus 20–21, Proverbs 30
March 13 - Matthew 14:22–36, Leviticus 22–23, Proverbs 31
March 14 - Matthew 15:1–20, Leviticus 24–25, Ecclesiastes 1:1–11
March 15 - Matthew 15:21–39, Leviticus 26–27, Ecclesiastes
    1:12–2:26
March 16 - Matthew 16, Numbers 1–2, Ecclesiastes 3:1–15
March 17 - Matthew 17, Numbers 3–4, Ecclesiastes 3:16–4:16
March 18 - Matthew 18:1–20, Numbers 5–6, Ecclesiastes 5
March 19 - Matthew 18:21–35, Numbers 7–8, Ecclesiastes 6
March 20 - Matthew 19:1–15, Numbers 9–10, Ecclesiastes 7
March 21 - Matthew 19:16–30, Numbers 11–12, Ecclesiastes 8
March 22 - Matthew 20:1–16, Numbers 13–14, Ecclesiastes
    9:1–12
March 23 - Matthew 20:17–34, Numbers 15–16, Ecclesiastes
    9:13–10:20
March 24 - Matthew 21:1–27, Numbers 17–18, Ecclesiastes
    11:1–8
March 25 - Matthew 21:28–46, Numbers 19–20, Ecclesiastes
    11:9–12:14
March 26 - Matthew 22:1–22, Numbers 21, Song of Solomon
    1:1–2:7

March 27 - MATTHEW 22:23–46, NUMBERS 22:1–40, SONG OF
SOLOMON 2:8-3:5

March 28 - MATTHEW 23:1–12, NUMBERS 22:41–23:26, SONG
OF SOLOMON 3:6–5:1

March 29 - MATTHEW 23:13–39, NUMBERS 23:27–24:25,
SONG OF SOLOMON 5:2–6:3

March 30 - MATTHEW 24:1–31, NUMBERS 25–27,
SONG OF SOLOMON 6:4–8:4

March 31 - MATTHEW 24:32–51, NUMBERS 28–29,
SONG OF SOLOMON 8:5–14

Bible Readings for April

April 1 - Matthew 25:1–30, Numbers 30–31, Job 1
April 2 - Matthew 25:31–46, Numbers 32–34, Job 2
April 3 - Matthew 26:1–25, Numbers 35–36, Job 3
April 4 - Matthew 26:26–46, Deuteronomy 1–2, Job 4
April 5 - Matthew 26:47–75, Deuteronomy 3–4, Job 5
April 6 - Matthew 27:1–31, Deuteronomy 5–6, Job 6
April 7 - Matthew 27:32–66, Deuteronomy 7–8, Job 7
April 8 - Matthew 28, Deuteronomy 9–10, Job 8
April 9 - Acts 1, Deuteronomy 11–12, Job 9
April 10 - Acts 2:1–13, Deuteronomy 13–14, Job 10
April 11 - Acts 2:14–47, Deuteronomy 15–16, Job 11
April 12 - Acts 3, Deuteronomy 17–18, Job 12
April 13 - Acts 4:1–22, Deuteronomy 19–20, Job 13
April 14 - Acts 4:23–37, Deuteronomy 21–22, Job 14
April 15 - Acts 5:1–16, Deuteronomy 23–24, Job 15
April 16 - Acts 5:17–42, Deuteronomy 25–27, Job 16
April 17 - Acts 6, Deuteronomy 28, Job 17
April 18 - Acts 7:1–22, Deuteronomy 29–30, Job 18
April 19 - Acts 7:23–60, Deuteronomy 31–32, Job 19
April 20 - Acts 8:1–25, Deuteronomy 33–34, Job 20
April 21 - Acts 8:26–40, Joshua 1–2, Job 21
April 22 - Acts 9:1–25, Joshua 3:1–5:1, Job 22
April 23 - Acts 9:26–43, Joshua 5:2–6:27, Job 23
April 24 - Acts 10:1–33, Joshua 7–8, Job 24
April 25 - Acts 10:34–48, Joshua 9–10, Job 25
April 26 - Acts 11:1–18, Joshua 11–12, Job 26
April 27 - Acts 11:19–30, Joshua 13–14, Job 27
April 28 - Acts 12, Joshua 15–17, Job 28
April 29 - Acts 13:1–25, Joshua 18–19, Job 29
April 30 - Acts 13:26–52, Joshua 20–21, Job 30

Bible Readings for May

May 1 - Acts 14, Joshua 22, Job 31
May 2 - Acts 15:1–21, Joshua 23–24, Job 32
May 3 - Acts 15:22–41, Judges 1, Job 33
May 4 - Acts 16:1–15, Judges 2–3, Job 34
May 5 - Acts 16:16–40, Judges 4–5, Job 35
May 6 - Acts 17:1–15, Judges 6, Job 36
May 7 - Acts 17:16–34, Judges 7–8, Job 37
May 8 - Acts 18, Judges 9, Job 38
May 9 - Acts 19:1–20, Judges 10:1–11:33, Job 39
May 10 - Acts 19:21–41, Judges 11:34–12:15, Job 40
May 11 - Acts 20:1–16, Judges 13, Job 41
May 12 - Acts 20:17–38, Judges 14–15, Job 42
May 13 - Acts 21:1–36, Judges 16, Psalm 42
May 14 - Acts 21:37–22:29, Judges 17–18, Psalm 43
May 15 - Acts 22:30–23:22, Judges 19, Psalm 44
May 16 - Acts 23:23–24:9, Judges 20, Psalm 45
May 17 - Acts 24:10–27, Judges 21, Psalm 46
May 18 - Acts 25, Ruth 1–2, Psalm 47
May 19 - Acts 26:1–18, Ruth 3–4, Psalm 48
May 20 - Acts 26:19–32, 1 Samuel 1:1–2:10, Psalm 49
May 21 - Acts 27:1–12, 1 Samuel 2:11–36, Psalm 50
May 22 - Acts 27:13–44, 1 Samuel 3, Psalm 51
May 23 - Acts 28:1–16, 1 Samuel 4–5, Psalm 52
May 24 - Acts 28:17–31, 1 Samuel 6–7, Psalm 53
May 25 - Romans 1:1–15, 1 Samuel 8, Psalm 54
May 26 - Romans 1:16–32, 1 Samuel 9:1–10:16, Psalm 55
May 27 - Romans 2:1–3:8, 1 Samuel 10:17–11:15, Psalm 56
May 28 - Romans 3:9–31, 1 Samuel 12, Psalm 57
May 29 - Romans 4, 1 Samuel 13, Psalm 58
May 30 - Romans 5, 1 Samuel 14, Psalm 59
May 31 - Romans 6, 1 Samuel 15, Psalm 60

Bible Readings for June

June 1 - Romans 7, 1 Samuel 16, Psalm 61
June 2 - Romans 8 1 Samuel 17:1–54, Psalm 62
June 3 - Romans 9:1–29, 1 Samuel 17:55–18:30, Psalm 63
June 4 - Romans 9:30–10:21, 1 Samuel 19, Psalm 64
June 5 - Romans 11:1–24, 1 Samuel 20, Psalm 65
June 6 - Romans 11:25–36, 1 Samuel 21–22, Psalm 66
June 7 - Romans 12, 1 Samuel 23–24, Psalm 67
June 8 - Romans 13, 1 Samuel 25, Psalm 68
June 9 - Romans 14, 1 Samuel 26, Psalm 69
June 10 - Romans 15:1–13, 1 Samuel 27–28, Psalm 70
June 11 - Romans 15:14–33, 1 Samuel 29–31, Psalm 71
June 12 - Romans 16, 2 Samuel 1, Psalm 72
June 13 - Mark 1:1–20, 2 Samuel 2:1–3:1, Daniel 1
June 14 - Mark 1:21–45, 2 Samuel 3:2–39, Daniel 2:1–23
June 15 - Mark 2, 2 Samuel 4–5, Daniel 2:24–49
June 16 - Mark 3:1–19, 2 Samuel 6, Daniel 3
June 17 - Mark 3:20–35, 2 Samuel 7–8, Daniel 4
June 18 - Mark 4:1–20, 2 Samuel 9–10, Daniel 5
June 19 - Mark 4:21–41, 2 Samuel 11–12, Daniel 6
June 20 - Mark 5:1–20, 2 Samuel 13, Daniel 7
June 21 - Mark 5:21–43, 2 Samuel 14, Daniel 8
June 22 - Mark 6:1–29, 2 Samuel 15, Daniel 9
June 23 - Mark 6:30–56, 2 Samuel 16, Daniel 10
June 24 - Mark 7:1–13, 2 Samuel 17, Daniel 11:1–19
June 25 - Mark 7:14–37, 2 Samuel 18, Daniel 11:20–45
June 26 - Mark 8:1–21, 2 Samuel 19, Daniel 12
June 27 - Mark 8:22–9:1, 2 Samuel 20–21, Hosea 1:1–2:1
June 28 - Mark 9:2–50, 2 Samuel 22, Hosea 2:2–23
June 29 - Mark 10:1–31, 2 Samuel 23, Hosea 3
June 30 - Mark 10:32–52, 2 Samuel 24, Hosea 4:1–11

BIBLE READINGS FOR JULY

July 1 - MARK 11:1–14, 1 KINGS 1, HOSEA 4:12–5:4
July 2 - MARK 11:15–33, 1 KINGS 2, HOSEA 5:5–15
July 3 - MARK 12:1–27, 1 KINGS 3, HOSEA 6:1–7:2
July 4 - MARK 12:28–44, 1 KINGS 4-5, HOSEA 7:3–16
July 5 - MARK 13:1–13, 1 KINGS 6, HOSEA 8
July 6 - MARK 13:14–37, 1 KINGS 7, HOSEA 9:1–16
July 7 - MARK 14:1–31, 1 KINGS 8, HOSEA 9:17–10:15
July 8 - MARK 14:32–72, 1 KINGS 9, HOSEA 11:1–11
July 9 - MARK 15:1–20, 1 KINGS 10, HOSEA 11:12–12:14
July 10 - MARK 15:21–47, 1 KINGS 11, HOSEA 13
July 11 - MARK 16, 1 KINGS 12:1–31, HOSEA 14
July 12 - 1 CORINTHIANS 1:1–17, 1 KINGS 12:32–13:34, JOEL 1
July 13 - 1 CORINTHIANS 1:18–31, 1 KINGS 14, JOEL 2:1–11
July 14 - 1 CORINTHIANS 2, 1 KINGS 15:1–32, JOEL 2:12–32
July 15 - 1 CORINTHIANS 3, 1 KINGS 15:33–16:34, JOEL 3
July 16 - 1 CORINTHIANS 4, 1 KINGS 17, AMOS 1
July 17 - 1 CORINTHIANS 5, 1 KINGS 18, AMOS 2:1–3:2
July 18 - 1 CORINTHIANS 6, 1 KINGS 19, AMOS 3:3–4:3
July 19 - 1 CORINTHIANS 7:1–24, 1 KINGS 20, AMOS 4:4–13
July 20 - 1 CORINTHIANS 7:25–40, 1 KINGS 21, AMOS 5
July 21 - 1 CORINTHIANS 8, 1 KINGS 22, AMOS 6
July 22 - 1 CORINTHIANS 9, 2 KINGS 1–2, AMOS 7
July 23 - 1 CORINTHIANS 10, 2 KINGS 3, AMOS 8
July 24 - 1 CORINTHIANS 11:1–16, 2 KINGS 4, AMOS 9
July 25 - 1 CORINTHIANS 11:17–34, 2 KINGS 5, OBADIAH
July 26 - 1 CORINTHIANS 12, 2 KINGS 6:1–7:2, JONAH 1
July 27 - 1 CORINTHIANS 13, 2 KINGS 7:3–20, JONAH 2
July 28 - 1 CORINTHIANS 14:1–25, 2 KINGS 8, JONAH 3
July 29 - 1 CORINTHIANS 14:26–40, 2 KINGS 9, JONAH 4
July 30 - 1 CORINTHIANS 15:1–34, 2 KINGS 10, MICAH 1
July 31 - 1 CORINTHIANS 15:35–58, 2 KINGS 11, MICAH 2

Bible Readings for August

August 1 - 1 Corinthians 16, 2 Kings 12–13, Micah 3

August 2 - 2 Corinthians 1:1–2:4, 2 Kings 14, Micah 4:1–5:1

August 3 - 2 Corinthians 2:5–3:18, 2 Kings 15–16, Micah 5:2–15

August 4 - 2 Corinthians 4:1–5:10, 2 Kings 17, Micah 6

August 5 - 2 Corinthians 5:11–6:13, 2 Kings 18, Micah 7

August 6 - 2 Corinthians 6:14–7:16, 2 Kings 19, Nahum 1

August 7 - 2 Corinthians 8, 2 Kings 20–21, Nahum 2

August 8 - 2 Corinthians 9, 2 Kings 22:1–23:35, Nahum 3

August 9 - 2 Corinthians 10, 2 Kings 23:36–24:20, Habakkuk 1

August 10 - 2 Corinthians 11, 2 Kings 25, Habakkuk 2

August 11 - 2 Corinthians 12, 1 Chronicles 1–2, Habakkuk 3

August 12 - 2 Corinthians 13, 1 Chronicles 3–4, Zephaniah 1

August 13 - John 1:1–18, 1 Chronicles 5–6, Zephaniah 2

August 14 - John 1:19–34, 1 Chronicles 7–8, Zephaniah 3

August 15 - John 1:35–51, 1 Chronicles 9, Haggai 1–2

August 16 - John 2, 1 Chronicles 10–11, Zechariah 1

August 17 - John 3:1–21, 1 Chronicles 12, Zechariah 2

August 18 - John 3:22–36, 1 Chronicles 13–14, Zechariah 3

August 19 - John 4:1–26, 1 Chronicles 15:1–16:6, Zechariah 4

August 20 - John 4:27–42, 1 Chronicles 16:7–43, Zechariah 5

August 21 - John 4:43–54, 1 Chronicles 17, Zechariah 6

August 22 - John 5:1–18, 1 Chronicles 18–19, Zechariah 7

August 23 - John 5:19–47, 1 Chronicles 20:1–22:1, Zechariah 8

August 24 - John 6:1–21, 1 Chronicles 22:2–23:32, Zechariah 9

August 25 - John 6:22–59, 1 Chronicles 24, Zechariah 10

August 26 - John 6:60–71, 1 Chronicles 25–26, Zechariah 11

August 27 - John 7:1–24, 1 Chronicles 27–28, Zechariah 12

August 28 - John 7:25–52, 1 Chronicles 29, Zechariah 13

August 29 - John 8:1–20, 2 Chronicles 1:1–2:16, Zechariah 14

August 30 - John 8:21–47, 2 Chronicles 2:17–5:1, Malachi 1:1–2:9

August 31 - John 8:48–59, 2 Chronicles 5:2–14, Malachi 2:10–16

Bible Readings for September

September 1 - JOHN 9:1–23, 2 CHRONICLES 6, MALACHI 2:17–3:18
September 2 - JOHN 9:24–41, 2 CHRONICLES 7, MALACHI 4
September 3 - JOHN 10:1–21, 2 CHRONICLES 8, PSALM 73
September 4 - JOHN 10:22–42, 2 CHRONICLES 9, PSALM 74
September 5 - JOHN 11:1–27, 2 CHRONICLES 10–11, PSALM 75
September 6 - JOHN 11:28–57, 2 CHRONICLES 12–13, PSALM 76
September 7 - JOHN 12:1–26, 2 CHRONICLES 14–15, PSALM 77
September 8 - JOHN 12:27–50, 2 CHRONICLES 16–17, PSALM 78:1–20
September 9 - JOHN 13:1–20, 2 CHRONICLES 18, PSALM 78:21–37
September 10 - JOHN 13:21–38, 2 CHRONICLES 19, PSALM 78:38–55
September 11 - JOHN 14:1–14, 2 CHRONICLES 20:1–21:1, PSALM
        78:56–72
September 12 - JOHN 14:15–31, 2 CHRONICLES 21:2–22:12, PSALM 79
September 13 - JOHN 15:1–16:4, 2 CHRONICLES 23, PSALM 80
September 14 - JOHN 16:4–33, 2 CHRONICLES 24, PSALM 81
September 15 - JOHN 17, 2 CHRONICLES 25, PSALM 82
September 16 - JOHN 18:1–18, 2 CHRONICLES 26, PSALM 83
September 17 - JOHN 18:19–38, 2 CHRONICLES 27–28, PSALM 84
September 18 - JOHN 18:38–19:16, 2 CHRONICLES 29, PSALM 85
September 19 - JOHN 19:16–42, 2 CHRONICLES 30, PSALM 86
September 20 - JOHN 20:1–18, 2 CHRONICLES 31, PSALM 87
September 21 - JOHN 20:19–31, 2 CHRONICLES 32, PSALM 88
September 22 - JOHN 21, 2 CHRONICLES 33, PSALM 89:1–18
September 23 - 1 JOHN 1, 2 CHRONICLES 34, PSALM 89:19–37
September 24 - 1 JOHN 2, 2 CHRONICLES 35, PSALM 89:38–52
September 25 - 1 JOHN 3, 2 CHRONICLES 36, PSALM 90
September 26 - 1 JOHN 4, EZRA 1–2, PSALM 91
September 27 - 1 JOHN 5, EZRA 3–4, PSALM 92
September 28 - 2 JOHN, EZRA 5–6, PSALM 93
September 29 - 3 JOHN, EZRA 7–8, PSALM 94
September 30 - JUDE, EZRA 9–10, PSALM 95

Bible Readings for October

October 1 - Revelation 1, Nehemiah 1–2, Psalm 96
October 2 - Revelation 2, Nehemiah 3, Psalm 97
October 3 - Revelation 3, Nehemiah 4, Psalm 98
October 4 - Revelation 4, Nehemiah 5:1–7:4, Psalm 99
October 5 - Revelation 5, Nehemiah 7:5–8:12, Psalm 100
October 6 - Revelation 6, Nehemiah 8:13–9:37, Psalm 101
October 7 - Revelation 7, Nehemiah 9:38–10:39, Psalm 102
October 8 - Revelation 8, Nehemiah 11, Psalm 103
October 9 - Revelation 9, Nehemiah 12, Psalm 104:1–23
October 10 - Revelation 10, Nehemiah 13, Psalm 104:24–35
October 11 - Revelation 11, Esther 1, Psalm 105:1–25
October 12 - Revelation 12, Esther 2, Psalm 105:26–45
October 13 - Revelation 13, Esther 3–4, Psalm 106:1–23
October 14 - Revelation 14, Esther 5:1–6:13, Psalm 106:24–48
October 15 - Revelation 15, Esther 6:14–8:17, Psalm 107:1–22
October 16 - Revelation 16, Esther 9–10, Psalm 107:23–43
October 17 - Revelation 17, Isaiah 1–2, Psalm 108
October 18 - Revelation 18, Isaiah 3–4, Psalm 109:1–19
October 19 - Revelation 19, Isaiah 5–6, Psalm 109:20–31
October 20 - Revelation 20, Isaiah 7–8, Psalm 110
October 21 - Revelation 21–22, Isaiah 9–10, Psalm 111
October 22 - 1 Thessalonians 1, Isaiah 11–13, Psalm 112
October 23 - 1 Thessalonians 2:1–16, Isaiah 14–16, Psalm 113
October 24 - 1 Thessalonians 2:17–3:13, Isaiah 17–19, Psalm 114
October 25 - 1 Thessalonians 4, Isaiah 20–22, Psalm 115
October 26 - 1 Thessalonians 5, Isaiah 23–24, Psalm 116
October 27 - 2 Thessalonians 1, Isaiah 25–26, Psalm 117
October 28 - 2 Thessalonians 2, Isaiah 27–28, Psalm 118
October 29 - 2 Thessalonians 3, Isaiah 29–30, Psalm 119:1–32
October 30 - 1 Timothy 1, Isaiah 31–33, Psalm 119:33–64
October 31 - 1 Timothy 2, Isaiah 34–35, Psalm 119:65–96

Bible Readings for November

November 1 - 1 Timothy 3, Isaiah 36–37, Psalm 119:97–120
November 2 - 1 Timothy 4, Isaiah 38–39, Psalm 119:121–144
November 3 - 1 Timothy 5:1–22, Jeremiah 1–2, Psalm 119:145–176
November 4 - 1 Timothy 5:23–6:21, Jeremiah 3–4, Psalm 120
November 5 - 2 Timothy 1, Jeremiah 5–6, Psalm 121
November 6 - 2 Timothy 2, Jeremiah 7–8, Psalm 122
November 7 - 2 Timothy 3, Jeremiah 9–10, Psalm 123
November 8 - 2 Timothy 4, Jeremiah 11–12, Psalm 124
November 9 - Titus 1, Jeremiah 13–14, Psalm 125
November 10 - Titus 2, Jeremiah 15–16, Psalm 126
November 11 - Titus 3, Jeremiah 17–18, Psalm 127
November 12 - Philemon, Jeremiah 19–20, Psalm 128
November 13 - James 1, Jeremiah 21–22, Psalm 129
November 14 - James 2, Jeremiah 23–24, Psalm 130
November 15 - James 3, Jeremiah 25–26, Psalm 131
November 16 - James 4, Jeremiah 27–28, Psalm 132
November 17 - James 5, Jeremiah 29–30, Psalm 133
November 18 - 1 Peter 1, Jeremiah 31–32, Psalm 134
November 19 - 1 Peter 2, Jeremiah 33–34, Psalm 135
November 20 - 1 Peter 3, Jeremiah 35–36, Psalm 136
November 21 - 1 Peter 4, Jeremiah 37–38, Psalm 137
November 22 - 1 Peter 5, Jeremiah 39–40, Psalm 138
November 23 - 2 Peter 1, Jeremiah 41–42, Psalm 139
November 24 - 2 Peter 2, Jeremiah 43–44, Psalm 140
November 25 - 2 Peter 3, Jeremiah 45–46, Psalm 141
November 26 - Galatians 1, Jeremiah 47–48, Psalm 142
November 27 - Galatians 2, Jeremiah 49–50, Psalm 143
November 28 - Galatians 3:1–18, Jeremiah 51–52, Psalm 144
November 29 - Galatians 3:19–4:20, Lamentations 1–2, Psalm 145
November 30 - Galatians 4:21–31, Lamentations 3–4, Psalm 146

BIBLE READINGS FOR DECEMBER

December 1 - GALATIANS 5:1–15, LAMENTATIONS 5, PSALM 147
December 2 - GALATIANS 5:16–26, EZEKIEL 1, PSALM 148
December 3 - GALATIANS 6, EZEKIEL 2–3, PSALM 149
December 4 - EPHESIANS 1, EZEKIEL 4–5, PSALM 150
December 5 - EPHESIANS 2, EZEKIEL 6–7, ISAIAH 40
December 6 - EPHESIANS 3, EZEKIEL 8–9, ISAIAH 41
December 7 - EPHESIANS 4:1–16, EZEKIEL 10–11, ISAIAH 42
December 8 - EPHESIANS 4:17–32, EZEKIEL 12–13, ISAIAH 43
December 9 - EPHESIANS 5:1–20, EZEKIEL 14–15, ISAIAH 44
December 10 - EPHESIANS 5:21–33, EZEKIEL 16, ISAIAH 45
December 11 - EPHESIANS 6, EZEKIEL 17, ISAIAH 46
December 12 - PHILIPPIANS 1:1–11, EZEKIEL 18, ISAIAH 47
December 13 - PHILIPPIANS 1:12–30, EZEKIEL 19, ISAIAH 48
December 14 - PHILIPPIANS 2:1–11, EZEKIEL 20, ISAIAH 49
December 15 - PHILIPPIANS 2:12–30, EZEKIEL 21–22, ISAIAH 50
December 16 - PHILIPPIANS 3, EZEKIEL 23, ISAIAH 51
December 17 - PHILIPPIANS 4, EZEKIEL 24, ISAIAH 52
December 18 - COLOSSIANS 1:1–23, EZEKIEL 25–26, ISAIAH 53
December 19 - COLOSSIANS 1:24–2:19, EZEKIEL 27–28, ISAIAH 54
December 20 - COLOSSIANS 2:20–3:17, EZEKIEL 29–30, ISAIAH 55
December 21 - COLOSSIANS 3:18–4:18, EZEKIEL 31–32, ISAIAH 56
December 22 - LUKE 1:1–25, EZEKIEL 33, ISAIAH 57
December 23 - LUKE 1:26–56, EZEKIEL 34, ISAIAH 58
December 24 - LUKE 1:57–80, EZEKIEL 35–36, ISAIAH 59
December 25 - LUKE 2:1–20, EZEKIEL 37, ISAIAH 60
December 26 - LUKE 2:21–52, EZEKIEL 38–39, ISAIAH 61
December 27 - LUKE 3:1–20, EZEKIEL 40–41, ISAIAH 62
December 28 - LUKE 3:21–38, EZEKIEL 42–43, ISAIAH 63
December 29 - LUKE 4:1–30, EZEKIEL 44–45, ISAIAH 64
December 30 - LUKE 4:31–44, EZEKIEL 46–47, ISAIAH 65
December 31 - LUKE 5:1–26, EZEKIEL 48, ISAIAH 66